D0445592

THE
WIDOW'S
BLIND
DATE

THE WIDOW'S BLIND DATE

A PLAY BY
Israel Horovitz

GARDEN CITY, NY

Copyright © 1989 by Israel Horovitz

CAUTION: Professionals and amateurs are hereby warned that THE WIDOW'S BLIND DATE is subject to a royalty. It is fully protected under the copyright laws of the United States of America, and of all countries covered by the International Copyright Union (including the Dominion of Canada and the rest of the British Commonwealth), and of all countries covered by the Pan-American Copyright Convention and the Universal Copyright Convention, and of all countries with which the United States has reciprocal copyright relations. All rights, including professional, amateur, motion picture, recitation, lecturing, public reading, radio broadcasting, television, video or sound taping, all other forms of mechanical or electronic reproduction, such as information storage and retrieval systems and photocopying, and the rights of translation into foreign languages, are strictly reserved. Particular emphasis is laid upon the question of readings, permission for which must be secured from the author's agent in writing.

The stock and amateur production rights in THE WIDOW'S BLIND DATE are controlled exclusively by the DRAMATISTS PLAY SERVICE, INC., 440 Park Avenue South, New York, N.Y. 10016. No stock or amateur performance of the play may be given without obtaining in advance the written permission of the DRAMATISTS PLAY SERVICE, INC., and paying the requisite fee.

All inquiries concerning rights (other than stock and amateur rights) should be addressed to William Morris Agency, Inc., 1350 Avenue of the Americas, New York, N.Y. 10019, Attention: Samuel Liff.

Manufactured in the United States of America

Design by Maria Chiarino

Photographs by Peter Cunningham

Quality Printing and Binding by:
BERRYVILLE GRAPHICS
P.O. Box 272
Berryville, VA 22611 U.S.A.

For Anke
Barbara
Catherine
Chris
Diane
Dossy
Gill
Heidi
Jill
Kim
Patricia
Al
Bob
Biff
Bush
Charles
Christian
David
Ebbe
Frank
Frank
Götz
Grey
Hawk
Jacques
Olivier
Paul
Peter
Philippe
Pop
Tom,
and Uncle Max

THE WIDOW'S BLIND DATE was first produced in a staged reading by The New York Playwrights Lab under the auspices of The Actors Studio, featuring Jill Eikenberry, Robert Field and Ebbe Roe Smith, directed by Sheldon Larry. The play then had its World Premiere at the Los Angeles Theatre Center, featuring Frank McCarthy, Charlie Parks and Patricia Wettig, directed by Bill Bushnell. Subsequent major productions, prior to the play's NYC opening included: three separate productions at The Gloucester Stage Company, featuring Kim Armeen, Tom Bloom, Al Mohrmann, Paul O'Brien and Dossy Peabody, directed by Bill Bushnell, Grey Cattell Johnson and Israel Horovitz; the French premiere, featuring Catherine Gandois, Olivier Granier and Christian Rauth, directed by Philippe LeFebvre; and the German premiere, featuring Sebastian Koch, Frank Schroder and Anke Schubert, directed by Götz Burger.

THE WIDOW'S BLIND DATE opened on November 7, 1989 in New York City at Circle in the Square Downtown. It was produced by David Bulasky, Barbara Darwall and Peter von Mayrhauser. It was directed by Mr. Horovitz. The set was designed by Edward T. Gianfrancesco; lighting was designed by Craig Evans; costumes were designed by Janet Irving. The Production Stage Manager was Crystal Huntington. The cast was as follows:

Archie Crisp.	Paul O'Brien
George Ferguson	Tom Bloom
Margy Burke	Christine Estabrook

Scene: A newspaper baling plant in Wakefield, Massachusetts.

Time: The present. Saturday afternoon and evening, late
fall.

ACT I

5 p.m., Saturday afternoon, late fall, yellow light, slight chill in air.

A tinny–sounding radio plays "easy–listenin' " tunes.

Interior of baling press room. Large, high–ceilinged space with skylights and hanging, caged–in bare bulbs as light source.

Eight bales of newspaper stretch across the front edge of the stage, separating the audience from the stage. The bales will be removed in the opening minutes of the play by the actors, who, in a sense, "set the stage" and start the play.

A huge baling press is set upstage center of room: the main object. Stage right of the baler is a dune–like mound of loose newspapers from which armfuls of newspapers are carried to the press, into which they are loaded. Opposite side of baler, upstage, a small mountain of newspaper bundles tied with twine, stacked. A smaller mound of bundled newspaper is in evidence downstage right of baler. Loading doors are placed mid–stage right. 800–lb. bales of newspaper are in evidence all around perimeter of stage. Each bale is 4' wide by 3' thick by 4' high.

It is possible that a large hook and chain is suspended from ceiling, on a track. Also, a roller–track may be constructed in front of the baler to be used for propelling completed bales from baler to bale–stack.

A sharp–toothed hand truck is in evidence, also used for transporting bales from place to place in shop; and for loading doors on to truck for shipment to mills. N.B. If the stage is large enough, it is suggested that a gasoline or electricity powered "Towmotor" [forklift] be included among the scenery/props. Also, an enormous floor scale should be insinuated into the scenic plan, upstage right wall, so that completed bales can be shuttled by hand truck (or driven by Towmotor) across the scale, and weighed.

Upstage there is a locker, probably housing the radio. ARCHIE's *dress–up clothes: suit, shirt, tie, etc., are in evidence inside, as is* GEORGE's *jacket and scarf. There is an easy chair, probably a Barca–lounger, set downstage of the locker.*

The baling press should be large and ominous. A version of an old–fashioned wooden baler is wanted [c. 1940], with removable walls, a weighted, permanent base and adjustable top. Such a baler functions as follows: the press walls form an empty "box," which is filled with overissue newspapers or magazines. The top of the baler is fitted in place, steel oblong into side grooves more distant from top, causing top to squash overissues of magazines into a bale. When the proper size is achieved, men negotiate the tying of the bale with long black wire. When bale is tied, the steel oblongs are carefully removed from the baler's side–teeth and all sides and top are removed, causing the bale to stand alone. A roller–track is stored under the baler, slides out and is slotted into position at the baler's front door for bale removal. A hand truck is brought to the end of the roller–track and the bale is removed. The baler's front door and sides are replaced, the press is refilled, the process is repeated.

The lights come up on ARCHIE CRISP *and* GEORGE FERGUSON. ARCHIE *is in the midst of performing a story for* GEORGE, *who is enthralled. As* ARCHIE *tells his story, he moves the bales upstage, clearing the audience's view of the front edge of the stage.*

ARCHIE: So, this jamoca thinks he can take me real fast, throws a left and I roll under and come up from down like a fuckin' toad, George . . . and I throw my two arms out wicked straight and yell, "Whooooo–eeee!" . . . and he looks left and right . . . and I butt this jamoca with the top of my head and he is out! O.U.T. !

(ARCHIE *continues to move the remainder of the eight bales upstage, lining them up neatly like soldiers, ready to be tagged, weighed and loaded onto an imagined truck, presumably outside the loading doors offstage.*

GEORGE *sweeps, cleans.* NOTE: ARCHIE's *work must be substantial, authoritative: the boss's work.* GEORGE's *labor, by contrast, is menial, unimportant: the helper's work.*

They both swig beer from cans as they work and chat)

GEORGE: How many bales we got now?

ARCHIE: Counting the one we're working on, five, plus the two corrugated . . . seven . . . so's we need one more after this. Then we still got to tag 'em and run 'em over the scale and weigh 'em before we load. (*Pauses*) I might have'ta go away and come back.

GEORGE: We loadin' tonight?

ARCHIE: Use your head, will ya'? You can't leave a load out there all night. It's an open truck, the night air gets into these bales, they'll weigh twice as much in the morning.

GEORGE: I don't mind stickin' now, for the sortin' and weighin' part . . . I mean, I ain't got too much goin' in the plans–for–tonight department . . .

ARCHIE: Oh, yuh, well, I got kind of a supper thing I gotta do . . . I'm on for supper with Margy . . .

GEORGE: Margy? (GEORGE *turns radio off*) Swede's sistah, Margy?

ARCHIE: Oh, yuh, yuh. I bumped into her down Mal's Jewel Craft a while back. She called me up . . . to have supper with her.

GEORGE: She called you up?

ARCHIE: Oh, yuh, well, yuh, she did, yuh . . .

GEORGE: Jees! Still the aggressive one, Margy, huh?

ARCHIE: Oh, well, yuh, I guess . . .

GEORGE: I read in the paper she was comin' ta town. Swede's finally dyin', huh?

ARCHIE: She said that, yuh. Bad shape, yuh.

GEORGE: She's up and done som'pin' famous, I guess, huh? You read it in the *Item*?

ARCHIE: Me? Naw. Never touch a paper after I leave here. I get my fill, sorta, I guess . . . this line of work 'n' all . . .

GEORGE (*laughing*): I even clipped the article to show you. I can't God damn believe it, Arch! It's unbelievable! You got supper going with Swede's sistah?

ARCHIE: Hey listen, huh, ya know? Sure . . . sure! Swede Palumbo's sister Margy. She finds me . . . attractive.

GEORGE: Oh, yuh? Maybe she can find you a *job*! (*Laughs*) Where're you pickin' her up? 33 Elm?

ARCHIE: Uh–uh. She's pickin' *me* up here, 6:00 sharp.

GEORGE: *Here*?

ARCHIE: Yuh, here. Somethin' the matter with here?

GEORGE: It's a junk shop, for Christ's sake. (*Laughs*) Boy, you really got 'em hoppin' for you, Arch . . . I gotta hand it to ya . . . Pickin' him up at his God damn junk shop . . . What a guy . . . (*Laughs*) Hey, maybe you could send her over ta my place later, huh? For old time's sake . . .

ARCHIE (*twisting* GEORGE's *arm, forcing him to the ground*): Take it back! Take it back! Ya *derr*!

GEORGE: Lemme up, ya jerk!

ARCHIE: Take it back, take it back!

GEORGE: *Archie . . . God damn it . . . GOD DAMN IT, Archie!*

ARCHIE: You take it back?

GEORGE: Okay, yuh, okay, yuh, I take it back. (*Pauses*)

ARCHIE (*Releasing* GEORGE): You're free. Let's finish this bale, huh?

GEORGE (*standing, rubbing arms*): Top of your head, huh?

ARCHIE: I split his jaw.

GEORGE: Any bleeding?

ARCHIE: Why? You thirsty, or som'pin'?

(*There is a pause in the chat. The men work, wordlessly.* GEORGE *re–starts the conversation*)

GEORGE: Blind–Peter–Holier–Than–Fucking–Thou–Palumbo . . . never liked the peckah . . .

ARCHIE: Which one of us did?

GEORGE: You gonna try to get anything off her?

ARCHIE: Who?

GEORGE: Swede's sistah.

ARCHIE: Margy? (*Pauses*) Nothin' ta get. She's flatter'n a pancake . . . two raisins on a breadboard.

GEORGE: Carpenter's dream: flat as a board, easy to screw.

ARCHIE: Pirate's delight: sunken chest.

GEORGE: She ain't so bad.

ARCHIE: You were lookin'? You were peekin'? You were snoopin' in between the buttons when she stretches? You were watchin' her take off her coat . . . on the arms–behind–the–back part . . . when the two of them were shoved right out there . . . on view for all? That what you were doin', George?

GEORGE: Who? *Me?*

ARCHIE: Just us balin' here, right? I mean, I ain't seen nobody else pressin' these bales, right? Just you and me . . .

GEORGE: Yuh, I've thought about it now and again. But I haven't seen her in twenty years, Arch.

ARCHIE: How come you never moved on her?

GEORGE: On Swede's sistah?

ARCHIE: You sufferin' from a sho't memory problem, or what?

GEORGE: I never moved on Swede's sistah on accounta she was married. Also counta Swede. Also on accounta I haven't actually seen her since high school.

ARCHIE: She ain't been married in years and years!

GEORGE: Even worse. Widows give me the creeps, ya know. I look at her and her kids, and all's I can think about is what's–his–name dyin' an' all. . . . What's his name?

ARCHIE: You know, what's–his–name.

GEORGE: What's his name?

ARCHIE (*trying to remember*): What's his name? . . . *Don't tell me!* Don't tell me! . . . I got it! I got it! (*Suddenly*) Cootie!

GEORGE: Cootie Webber?

ARCHIE: Wasn't that him?

GEORGE: Are you nuts? Cootie Webber never married Swede's sistah. 'Sides . . . ain't Cootie Webber still alive?

ARCHIE: You crazy? Cootie Webber got hit by lightning . . . head of the lake.

GEORGE: You out of your mind? Cootie Webber ate bad clams.

ARCHIE: You off your gourd? (*Turns and faces* GEORGE) A woman's got a right to take off her coat, same as a

man, when she comes in. The world's changed, in
case ya haven't noticed! You got no right to be starin'
at her like she's public property, anymore, 'cause she
ain't. You get me? *Get me?*

GEORGE (*after a long pause*): You're really gone on her,
huh?

ARCHIE: I like her.

GEORGE: It doesn't give you the willies . . . that she's
got one husband in the grave . . . and kids? That
doesn't give you the willies, Arch?

ARCHIE: Death is a part of life, the way I see it.

GEORGE: No doubt about it.

ARCHIE: A widow's got a right to go out with me . . .
same as a non–widow.

GEORGE: I can see that.

ARCHIE: I like her.

GEORGE: I never stared.

ARCHIE: I never said you did.

GEORGE: I mean, I noticed she was good–lookin' and
all . . .

ARCHIE: Kinda flat–chested, though . . .

GEORGE: It's a gland, that's all. For feeding babies. I mean, how excited can a person get over a gland, right? You know what I mean? You follow me?

ARCHIE: I like 'em, myself.

GEORGE: Margy's, or in general?

ARCHIE: In general, I like 'em to be more ample than Margy's . . . I like them in general . . . to be more ample than . . . what Margy has to offer.

GEORGE: I was thinkin'. If Swede heard us going on about his sistah this way, we'd be goners, right.

ARCHIE: What are you? Nuts or something?

GEORGE: He's got a temper, Swede . . .

ARCHIE: The man's dyin', George. What have you got goin' upstairs? Mashed potatoes? 'Cause there sure ain't no gray matter up there!

GEORGE: All's I'm sayin' here is, "ya never know!" . . . Dyin' or not, Swede Palumbo wouldn't've shed a tear if the school bus run us down . . . and that's a fact . . . (Smiles) Course, it's *you* he really hates, ain't it?

ARCHIE: What's this?

GEORGE: Senior class beach party . . . what was Swede yellin', poor blind son–of–a–bitch? "I'm gonna kill you, Billy–Goat Crisp! I'm gonna kill you dead! Billy–Goat's gonna die!" Ain't that right?

ARCHIE: If you spill one word about this in front of Margy, I'll kill you, George!

GEORGE: What are you? Kidding? You don't think it's gonna come up?

ARCHIE: I'll be the judge of what stays down and what comes up. You get me? (GEORGE *giggles*) I don't hear an answer here, George. (GEORGE *laughs*) I wanna hear an answer, you! (GEORGE *tries to stop his laugh, but a fresh laugh explodes from him.* ARCHIE *is enraged*) I'm gonna butt your jaw with the top of my head . . .

GEORGE: C'mon, Arch, it just stands ta reason . . .

ARCHIE: Nothin' stands ta reason, you get me? You open your mouth one time on that subject and you won't be standin' to piss, let alone standin' to reason! You follow me, George? Huh?

GEORGE: Okay, okay!

ARCHIE: I'll hav'ta kill ya', otherwise . . .

GEORGE: I just said "okay," okay?

ARCHIE (*after a pause*): Okay.

GEORGE (*an involuntary giggle*): Heee . . . (*Shows palms to* ARCHIE) Just a laugh.

ARCHIE: And you keep your eyes to yourself, you hear me?

GEORGE: Honest to Christ, Arch, I never once looked. Cross my heart.

ARCHIE: Cross your ass, George! I don't like what I'm hearing from you, George, ya know that? There must be ten thousand different women around, ya know, if you add up Wakefield, Reading, Stoneham, Melrose and Woburn. You got no right to be movin' in where I'm having supper tonight.

GEORGE: God strike me dead if I'm movin' in, Arch.

ARCHIE: You better mean what you say.

GEORGE: I mean what I say. God strike me dead, and that's a fact. (*Pauses*) Don't you worry. (*Smiles*) I wouldn't add in Woburn women, if I were you, though.

ARCHIE (*smiles*): True enough.

GEORGE: Woburn women are dogs.

ARCHIE: The worst.

GEORGE: Pigs.

ARCHIE: The lowest.

GEORGE: I wouldn't touch 'em on a bet.

ARCHIE: Rot your hand.

GEORGE: Remember Ax Landry?

ARCHIE: The skinny one?

GEORGE: Went with Rufus What's'it's Woburn
cousin . . .

ARCHIE: The fat one with the wigs?

GEORGE: Remember?

ARCHIE (*hooting with laughter*): Who could forget?

GEORGE: Ax. Dumb fuck.

ARCHIE: Wicked dumb.

GEORGE: His sister, Dixie Cups . . . she had a mouth
like a toilet, huh?

ARCHIE: Wicked awful.

GEORGE: She says to me one night, up by the band-
stand, lookin' out at Lake Quannapowitt . . . sum-
mer . . . peaceful . . . sittin' on the grass . . . me
with my arm around her . . . thinkin', peaceful . . .
she says to me . . . (*Changes his posture, now in
imitation of Dixie Cups Landry*) "A lot of people
wonder why I wear cotton underpants."

ARCHIE: What?

GEORGE: I swear ta Christ, Arch! Outta nowhere this
broad is tellin' me a lot of people wonder why she
wears cotton underpants.

ARCHIE: You're makin' this up.

GEORGE: On my mother's grave . . .

ARCHIE: Ax Landry's sistah? (GEORGE *nods affirmatively*) I'll be dipped . . . (*Looks up*) What happened after?

GEORGE: After she said that? (*Smiles*) Well . . . (*Pauses*) The good part. I says, "How come?" And she says, "How come a lot of people wonder? Or how come I wear them?" (*Pauses, confidentially*) "How come you wear 'em?" I ask . . . quietlike . . . serious. (*Pauses*) "Ask me nicely," she says. So I do. "How come you wear cotton underpants, Mary Ellen?" I ask. She looks up, pokerface . . . (*Imitates her*) "So it can breathe," she says. "So *it* can breathe." (*Pauses, laughing, mock disgust*) Imagine, huh? Straight out, no shame, thinks this is funny. Ax Landry: his sistah.

ARCHIE: Dumb fuck. (*Standing, shaking leg*) C'mon, George, let's shake a leg. Get the roller, George.

GEORGE (*he moves to baler; works*): I, personally, would never take out a Woburn girl, even if she was the Pope's niece.

ARCHIE: There isn't a one of them that washes herself properly.

GEORGE: They never learned properly . . .

ARCHIE: It's all in the bringing up.

GEORGE: You said a mouthful.

ARCHIE: The manners. The washing and the scrubbing . . .

GEORGE: The don't talk back to your parents . . .

ARCHIE: The mind your manners . . .

GEORGE: The go to bed early and get up early . . .

ARCHIE: The you mind your tongue around your mother and your sistahs . . .

GEORGE: The honor thy father . . .

ARCHIE: The honor thy father . . . (*Pauses*) I do agree with you there, George. The honor thy father's the thing. (*Pauses, lost in memory. Then, quietly*) Jesus . . . I never figured when I was twelve and doin' this, that twenty/twenty–five years later I'd still be here, you know . . . doing this.

GEORGE: You could be doin' worse.

ARCHIE: Oh, yuh? what? (*Laughs. He rolls hand truck to base of roller–track*) Let's shake a leg here, huh?

(*He shakes his leg, doing the "shake a leg" joke a second time. He goes behind baler to shove bale forward and out of baler*)

GEORGE (*calls out to* ARCHIE): You always had the sense of humor, Arch. Even when you weren't funny . . .

(GEORGE *"shoulders" bale; waits for* ARCHIE's *help*)

ARCHIE (*running to* GEORGE. *Together, they guide bale down roller–track to hand truck. As they unload the bale, they chatter*): Careful . . .

GEORGE: Careful . . .

ARCHIE: Got it?

GEORGE: Yuh, yuh . . . let her go. . . . Careful!

ARCHIE: Careful!

GEORGE: Right. I got her!

(ARCHIE *rolls hand truck to line–up of bales; hurls bale forward and off hand truck, into stack. Then* ARCHIE *gets two beers from locker*)

ARCHIE: Bury the rollers. (GEORGE *does, wordlessly.* ARCHIE *continues*) Seven down, one to go. After this one, we got the overissue bale, then we just got the crap clean–up bale, George. Nothin' loose can be left in sight lyin' around. My Uncle Max goes apeshit if it ain't tidy when he gets in here mornin's. . . . So's anything here that isn't part of the building and don't have the strength to run away, up and in the baler! Like you. (ARCHIE *moves to* GEORGE, *pretending he's going to throw him up and into the baler.* GEORGE *rolls backwards into baler, giggling nervously.* AR-CHIE *has carried two beers with him. He shakes* GEORGE'*s can*) Here's a little reward for you, George. (*He opens it, spraying* GEORGE *with beer.* GEORGE *is delighted.*)

GEORGE: Heyyy!

ARCHIE: Early shower for you, kiddo. Lower that gate, George.

(*They drink beer awhile, tired, but pleased to be with one another*)

GEORGE: Where's this load goin'?

ARCHIE: Fitchburg. Felulah's Mill.

GEORGE: Wicked lotta drivin', huh?

ARCHIE: Oh, yuh, wicked. My uncle's outta here by 4:00 in the mornin'. . . . He hits Fitchburg by 6:00 or 7:00, gets unloaded by maybe 8:00, back here by 10:00, maybe 10:30. It's no fuckin' life for humans, I can tell ya that.

GEORGE: I never liked Fitchburg.

ARCHIE: Fitchburg never liked you, George.

GEORGE: Bunch of boozers.

ARCHIE: The worst.

GEORGE: Can't be trusted.

ARCHIE: All cons and ex-cons.

GEORGE: They'd steal yo'r eyeteeth.

ARCHIE: Fillings and all.

GEORGE: That's the truth.

ARCHIE: When's the last time we seen each other, George? Before the funeral? Three years ago?

GEORGE: Nearly, at the reunion.

ARCHIE: At the fifteenth?

GEORGE: Yup.

ARCHIE: Shit, time flies.

GEORGE: So, ah, where're ya takin' the widow for supper? Hazelwood?

ARCHIE: That's for me to know and you to find out.

GEORGE: Whoa!!

ARCHIE: I'd love to bullshit with ya' all night, but I gotta get this overissue bale done and get out of here. Okay?

GEORGE (*sipping his beer slowly, happily; sits back in chair, relaxing*): I'm enjoyin' this workin' with ya, Arch. I kid you not! This is enjoyable . . .

ARCHIE: Oh, yuh? Well, get to work!

(*They load paper into the baler awhile*)

ARCHIE: Well, ya know, George, sometimes it's life's tragedies that bring people closer than life's joys.

GEORGE: Well said, Arch . . .

ARCHIE: I ain't finished.

GEORGE: Sorry.

ARCHIE: Sometimes, George, it's the tragedy more than the joys of life that brings two guys like you and me back into close contact . . .

GEORGE: Yup, you were sayin' that . . .

ARCHIE: I mean, we've had our differences over the years, haven't we?

GEORGE: Oh, sure. . . . Many differences, Arch . . .

(*They pass each other carrying bundles to baler. Neither seems to take notice of what the other is saying*)

ARCHIE: I mean, I've really *hated* you, George . . . and with due cause . . . but when guys like us share the tragedy that we just have . . .

GEORGE: Oh, *I* see! You mean losin' Spike the Loon as we did . . .

ARCHIE: I never like hearin' people say "losin' " when they mean somebody died. It always seemed dumb ta me. Like when Pa died and people'd say, "Jees, Archie, you lost your Pa . . ." and I'd think ta myself: "Do they mean I lost him like in Filene's Bargain Basement kinda thing?"

GEORGE: Yuh, I guess, Just sayin' d–e–a–t–h out loud is kinda morbid, though . . .

ARCHIE: You gotta be able ta take the bad with the very bad . . . that's life . . .

GEORGE: I s'pose. There's the morbid with the very morbid . . .

ARCHIE: Right. The way Spike the Loon died was very morbid . . .

GEORGE: Gives me the willies . . .

ARCHIE: Spike the Loon worked for me and my Uncle Max, right here in this shop, ever since he flunked outta Salem State . . .

GEORGE: No great brain there . . .

ARCHIE: Why? You got the cancer cure figured out?

GEORGE: I was just sayin' Spike the Loon wasn't any genius . . .

ARCHIE: He was a friend.

GEORGE: I thought you couldn't stand him?

ARCHIE: That's only recent years . . .

GEORGE: Oh . . .

ARCHIE: See, George, you gotta live each day like it was your last . . .

GEORGE: I dunno . . .

ARCHIE: I know. That is an ancient Oriental philosophy. I heard it on WBZ, Sunday night . . . call–in show . . .

GEORGE: Japs called in?

ARCHIE (*glaring at* GEORGE, *angrily*): Jesus, you can be one aggravating son–of–a–bitch, George. What I'm tryin' ta do here is ta give you a compliment, but you're makin' it damn near impossible.

GEORGE: Sorry, Arch . . .

ARCHIE (*"toasting" him with beer can raised*): Look, I woulda be'n in real trouble gettin' this load out for my uncle for tomorrow, what with Spike the Loon dead and all . . . but . . . who's here ta help, no questions asked? Not a stranger but a former best buddy, 'cause that is life. Georgie K. Ferguson, townie and friend from his toes to his limp pecker to the top of his Boston Bruins stocking cap, right? This former best buddy looks across to Archie Crisp at the funeral of their mutual lifelong friend and co–worker, Spike the Loon, and asks if there is anything he can do ta help out at the shop. And I says "Yes" and here he is . . . helpin'. . . . Now that is worth more ta me than any rich bitch from Wakefield's Park section or Stoneham's Spot Pond district, and that is the God's–honest!

GEORGE (*sipping and tipping his beer*): I'm drinkin' ta that, Archie.

ARCHIE: Hop in, George.

GEORGE: I personally ain't be'n that close ta death before . . . I said the "D" word. (*Crosses himself*)

ARCHIE: Oh, Georgie.

GEORGE: Of course, there was a time I did stay too long
underwater . . .

ARCHIE: Takin' a swim in the lake?

GEORGE: Takin' a bath in the tub. (*Pauses*) I was little.
(*Pauses*) Trying to beat my brother's record. (*Pauses*)
We were competitive . . . with one another.

ARCHIE: I remember.

GEORGE: Takin' a bath. (*Pauses*) That was about as close
as I've come to it, I suppose. I watched my dog die
. . . Vergil . . . my cocker . . . I watched him die.
That was something to see . . . four hours it took
. . . Four hours and twenty–two minutes. (*Pauses*)
He died by the clock . . . in the pantry. (*Pauses*) I
watched *that*. (*Pauses*) God damn. God damn . . .

ARCHIE: I remember Vergil. Nice. Nice . . .

GEORGE: Hit by a '51 Studebaker. Squashed.

ARCHIE: I remember. . . . You told me.

GEORGE: '51 Studies looked the same front and back.
. . . You couldn't tell whether they were coming or
going. Vergil probably got confused.

ARCHIE: No doubt.

GEORGE: God damn.

ARCHIE: Nice little mutt.

GEORGE: They went bankrupt, too, those cars. They don't make 'em anymore. Gone! Off the face of the fucking earth!

ARCHIE: Not much of an idea, even then.

GEORGE: It would've be'n one thing, ya know, if he'd died right off the bat. But four hours and twenty–two minutes of painful excruciation? And for *what,* I ask you? For God damn *what?* Studebaker cars go totally fucking bankrupt and that is *it,* right? I mean Vergil is gone and so is the entire *brand!* This is beyond fucking ironic and tragic! This is definitely Robert–Frost–your–balls/seek–out–and–find–Studebaker himself and run him down. . . . Am I right on this?

ARCHIE: The good with the bad, George. Only natural. But you've gotta move on from it. You can't dwell on it. It's all a part of life. Part of life.

(MARGY PALUMBO *enters at the loading platform, behind the baler, far upstage, looking about nervously, confused*)

MARGY (*softly*): Archie Crisp?

GEORGE (*stays in baler, looks, taunts* ARCHIE *in grade-school way*): Hey, Archie, *somebody's* here! (*Sees* MARGY) Hey, Arch, look who's here.

ARCHIE: I see her! I see her! (ARCHIE *runs, grabs a towel to wipe ink smears and dirt from his skin. He pulls his suit jacket on over sleeveless undershirt. He is in a panic, trying to look presentable. He grabs his watch from locker shelf*) Christ, it's five pah'st six! We pissed away an hour! (ARCHIE *calls out to* MARGY) *Just a minute!*

GEORGE (*hiding in baler, peering out at* MARGY): Jesus, Arch, she got *old!*

ARCHIE (*upstage*): Shhh. C'mon, huh, George . . . Shut it, huh. She can hear and all. (*Calls out to* MARGY) Hey, Margy, down here. (*Worried, to* GEORGE) Mind your language, okay?

GEORGE: Sure, Arch, sure . . . no sweat . . . *no fuckin' sweat!*

(MARGY *enters baling press area; stands facing* ARCHIE *and* GEORGE. *She wears a full black skirt, long, black coat–sweater, full peasant–cut blouse, overbelted. She wears driving glasses, which she will soon remove. She carries a purse. Her car keys are still clutched in her hand*)

ARCHIE: Hey, Marg.

MARGY: Hello, Archie.

ARCHIE: How's it going? Long time, huh? How long since we saw each other—before Mal's the other day?

MARGY: Fifteen years, maybe, huh?

ARCHIE: Not that long. I saw you in Santuro's, buyin' subs . . . maybe ten/twelve years ago, after you, uh, lost your husband. You came back up here for the funeral and all. You remember seein' me?

MARGY: Did we talk?

ARCHIE: To each other? No! You remember George Ferguson?

(GEORGE *pops up like a puppet, in the baler*)

MARGY (*Seeing* GEORGE; *freezes. She stares blankly for a moment; doesn't seem to recognize* GEORGE): No, I'm sorry, I don't. Nice to meet you.

GEORGE: We went to school together.

MARGY: We did?

GEORGE: Sure. All twelve years. Georgie Ferguson? Gould Street? Up near the Stoneham line?

MARGY (*smiling at* GEORGE, *blankly*): No. Sorry. (*To* ARCHIE) Nice to see you again, Archie. Nice to see you.

ARCHIE: Nice yourself, Marg.

(*There is a short silence, which* GEORGE *will break*)

GEORGE (*still in baler*): There was a squirt–gun fight in second grade and you got hit in the face and you cried and told Mrs. Linder . . . you remember?

MARGY: I . . . I think so.

GEORGE: That was me. I squirted you.

MARGY: On purpose?

GEORGE: Accident.

MARGY: I remember.

GEORGE: George Ferguson. Second row, third seat in from the left . . . nearly in the middle . . .

MARGY: Yes, I think so . . . Georgie Ferguson . . . I think so . . . (*She smiles at* GEORGE)

GEORGE: Great ta see ya again, Margie. How's it goin'? (*There is another short silence*) How's Swede doin'?

ARCHIE: Hey, George! C'mon, huh?

MARGY: Swede's dying. They don't think he'll make it through the night tonight. He's dying. . . . That's why I'm here, right now . . .

GEORGE: In town?

MARGY: Hmmm?

GEORGE: Why you're here in Wakefield, or why you're here at Archie's Uncle Max's junk shop?

ARCHIE: Don't mind him. . . .

MARGY: I've been over at Melrose–Wakefield Hospital
since eight o'clock this morning. (*Pauses*) They've got
him on a respirator. (*Pauses*) I told the doctor I'd get
back there by eight-thirty or so. He's sleeping now.

(GEORGE *takes* MARGY'*s coat and pocketbook, puts
them in locker*)

GEORGE: Swede?

MARGY: Mmm. Swede.

ARCHIE: Well, now . . . that's a tragedy. (MARGIE *and*
GEORGE *both look at* ARCHIE *waiting for his move*)
Well . . . his age, huh? Death: That's the worst . . .
(*Looks at his shoes, silently*)

GEORGE (*confidently; smiling*): I remember Swede
when he could see . . .

(*There is another short silence*)

ARCHIE (*staring* GEORGE *down. Sits by* MARGIE *on
bale*): So, Margy . . . how're the kids doin'?

MARGY: Fine.

ARCHIE: How many you got now?

MARGY: Same as ever.

ARCHIE: Five?

MARGY: Two. (*Pauses*) Rosie and Raymond.

ARCHIE: Little Cootie?

MARGY: I beg your pardon?

ARCHIE: Your son?

MARGY (*smiling quizzically*): I don't understand.

GEORGE (*Moving a bale down center and sitting*): Your boy. . . . Your son. Archie thinks you were married to Cootie Webber.

ARCHIE: Wasn't that him?

MARGY: My husband?

ARCHIE: Yuh.

MARGY: Who is Cootie Webber?

ARCHIE: He wasn't your ex?

MARGY: Edgar Burke.

ARCHIE: Your husband?

MARGY: Passed away twelve years ago.

ARCHIE: Sorry to hear that.

MARGY: The children were still babies. Raymond was only three months old; Rosie was two and a half.

GEORGE: You didn't waste much time, did you?

MARGY: Hmmm?

GEORGE: Havin' the kiddoes. You didn't waste your time.

ARCHIE: What are you sayin', George?

GEORGE: I was just telling Margy here that I could see she didn't waste any of her valuable time . . . waiting to get right down to have the little ones. She got right down to it . . . (*To* MARGY) Didn'tcha?

MARGY: We waited two years.

GEORGE: How old are you now?

MARGY: Nearly thirty–seven . . . soon.

GEORGE (*walking around space while calculating*): Twelve years since he died . . . add two for the kid is fourteen . . . plus nine months for the being pregnant and all . . . that's fifteen . . . plus the two you waited . . . is seventeen . . . that makes you about twenty when you hooked up with him.

ARCHIE: You didn't go to college?

GEORGE: I thought you were in the college course?

ARCHIE: You didn't get accepted?

GEORGE: You change your plans or what?

MARGY: I went to college.

GEORGE: For just a year?

ARCHIE: Junior college or a regular full college?

MARGY: Boston State.

GEORGE: Boston Teachers?

MARGY: Well . . . yes.

ARCHIE: You a teacher?

MARGY: No . . .

ARCHIE: You had to quit teaching when you were having your babies, huh?

MARGY: No, I finished. We waited.

GEORGE: Oh. right.

ARCHIE: Right.

GEORGE: I couldn't figure how you could've done both, ya know what I mean. Teachers can't have babies . . .

MARGY: Now they can.

GEORGE: Uh–uh.

MARGY: They can. The rule changed. They changed the rule.

ARCHIE: Is that a fact?

MARGY: It is.

ARCHIE: I wouldn't want my teacher to be having her own children.

GEORGE: Me, neither. (*Sits on bale*)

ARCHIE: They've got no need.

(MARGIE *looks at* ARCHIE, *quizzically*)

ARCHIE: They've got all us kids, anyway: you, me, George . . .

GEORGE: Swede, Cootie, Delbert . . .

ARCHIE: Delbert! (*Laughs*)

GEORGE: What did you say his name was? (MARGY *looks at* GEORGE, *blankly*) Your husband's.

MARGY: Edgar's?

GEORGE: Yuh.

MARGY: Edgar's name?

GEORGE: Yuh.

MARGY: You want to know what Edgar's *name* was?

GEORGE: Yuh.

MARGY: Edgar's name was Edgar.

GEORGE (*annoyed; a childish tone*): His *lah'st* name!

MARGY: Oh. I see. You mean Edgar's *sur*name. Your question was unclear. (*Pauses*) Burke.

ARCHIE: Related to Doctor Burke?

MARGY: Oh, yes, Doctor Burke . . . top of Prospect Street . . . Nope, uh–uh. Edgar came from different Burkes.

ARCHIE: Greenwood?

MARGY: Uh–uh. Edgar's family's from Woodville District . . .

GEORGE: Oh, yuh? *Burke?*

MARGY: Why do you *doubt* me, George? The name was Burke.

GEORGE: What did the father do?

MARGY: Edgar's? Oh, well, he worked . . . head of the lake.

ARCHIE: Filling station?

MARGY: Uh, no . . .

GEORGE: Lakeside Furniture?

MARGY: Cemetery.

ARCHIE: Oh, yuh? Doin' what?

MARGY: Well, uh, lawn care.

ARCHIE: Oh, yuh? Lawn care, huh?

GEORGE: You mean graves and all?

MARGY: Well, yuh, that, too . . .

GEORGE: Lawn care and digging kind of thing?

MARGY: I guess.

ARCHIE: Oh, yuh?

GEORGE: Willies: That's what this gives me. I swear to Christ!

MARGY: Hmmm?

ARCHIE: What are you driving these days, Marg?

MARGY: Me?

ARCHIE: A Chrysler LeBaron?

MARGY: No.

GEORGE: A Ford Mustang?

ARCHIE: Somethin' big?

GEORGE: A Pontiac Monte Carlo?

MARGY: No.

GEORGE: Maybe one of those Jap jobs! A Toyota? A Nissan?

ARCHIE: Mitsubishi?

GEORGE: Subaru!

ARCHIE: Mazda!

GEORGE: Isuzu!

MARGY: My husband's father's car. . . . That's what I'm driving: my husband's father's car.

ARCHIE: No kidding?

MARGY: Ancient.

GEORGE: Model–T sort of thing?

ARCHIE: Something classic?

MARGY: '51 Studebaker . . . two door . . . (*Smiles*) Powder blue . . . (*smiles again*) You can't tell the front from the back. (*Pauses*) I can't, anyway. . . . I'm always opening the trunk to check the oil. That sort of thing. Wicked funny . . . odd . . . unique, though, if you like that sort of thing.

GEORGE: Do you?

MARGY: Hmmm?

GEORGE: Like that sort of thing?

MARGY: The Studie? Sure. I love it. Makes me feel . . . nice. (*She giggles*) I'm always opening the trunk to check the oil.

ARCHIE: Was he kinda skinny?

MARGY: The antecedent to the pronoun "he" is not precisely clear, Archie. Do you mean my father–in–law? Was my father–in–law skinny?

ARCHIE: Well, no. Your *husbin'*. . . . Is your husbin' skinny?

MARGY: Is my husband skinny? My husband has been dead and in his grave for twelve years, Archie! Don't you find the question, "Is he skinny?" rather *grim*?

ARCHIE: I didn't mean "is." I meant "was."

MARGY: Oh, was.

ARCHIE: In high school.

MARGY: Was my husband skinny in high school? (*Pauses*) Oh, I see . . . (*Considers this*) I suppose. He was more tall than skinny . . .

GEORGE: He play ball?

ARCHIE: Naw, I woulda known him . . .

GEORGE: Basketball, I mean . . .

ARCHIE: I woulda known him, George. I knew everybody.

GEORGE: Was he definitely our year, Marg?

MARGY: Definitely.

GEORGE: I'll hav'ta look it up . . . in the yearbook.

ARCHIE: How come you never came to any of our reunions?

MARGY: Our what?

ARCHIE: Our reunions.

GEORGE: Our reunions.

MARGY: Oh, well . . . I just didn't.

GEORGE: Didn't want to.

MARGY: Yes. I didn't want to.

ARCHIE: How come? They were pretty rich.

MARGY: I'll just bet they were!

GEORGE: They were good . . .

ARCHIE: They were fun . . .

GEORGE: Good to see the old gang sort of thing . . .
(*Gets up to play with* ARCHIE *at center*)

ARCHIE: Makes you laugh.

GEORGE: Shadow Flint, with his weird hats . . .

ARCHIE: "Longest Hair?" Fred who's'its . . . (*He moves toward* GEORGE)

GEORGE: "Longest Distance Traveled?" . . . Arthur, the Jew . . .

ARCHIE: "Most Kids?" . . . remember who?

GEORGE: Maureen . . .

ARCHIE: And Whopp'ah . . . every reunion . . .

GEORGE: Started right away . . .

ARCHIE: Spike the Loon used ta always say Whopp'ah nailed Maureen first time while they were still in their caps and gowns . . .

GEORGE: "Most Kids" by a mile. . . . Every reunion . . .

ARCHIE: Wicked devout Catholics . . .

GEORGE: Makes you laugh . . .

ARCHIE (*laughing*): You missed a couple of great ones, Marg . . . the fifth . . .

GEORGE: The tenth was better . . .

ARCHIE: The tenth was good, too . . . The fifteenth was great! (*Laughs*) The twentieth comin' up soon, too . . .

MARGY: Maybe I'll peek in . . .

ARCHIE: You gotta see it ta believe it . . .

GEORGE: Unbelievable . . .

ARCHIE: Everybody lookin' awful . . .

GEORGE: Beer bellies . . .

ARCHIE: Bald . . .

GEORGE: Some dead, even . . . (ARCHIE *stares at* GEORGE; *a pause*) Sorry, Marg, huh?

ARCHIE: He didn't mean anything. Did you, Georgie?

MARGY: It's okay . . .

GEORGE: I'm really sorry . . .

MARGY: It's *okay*. (*Pauses*) *Ree*ally. (*Pauses*) I'll need a date.

ARCHIE: For the twentieth? (*She smiles*) Should be no sweat for you, Marg . . . (*He smiles*) Good–lookin' girl . . .

GEORGE: Got her own car and all . . .

ARCHIE: No sweat at all. Not at all . . .

GEORGE: I wouldn't mind takin' ya myself, Marg . . .

MARGY (*darkly*) Oh, okay, George. It's a date . . .

GEORGE: Hey! Well! Great!

ARCHIE: That s'posed ta be funny?

GEORGE: Naw. . . . Just kidding, Arch.

ARCHIE: I don't find that kind of kiddin' too ho–ho–that's–rich funny, George.

GEORGE: Meant no harm, Arch.

ARCHIE: *Not funny now, not funny then!*

GEORGE: C'mon, Arch . . .

ARCHIE (*goes to* GEORGE *to confront him*): What is it? In your blood? Or *what*? You out of control or som'pin'? Or *what*?

GEORGE: You startin' in again, Arnold?

ARCHIE (*to* MARGY): I go back a ways with this one, Marg. (*Pauses*) We got a history. (*Pauses*) All the ways back to West Ward School. . . . I shoulda known then, I swear ta Christ! (*Pauses*) A history. George Ferguson messing with Archie Crisp's girls . . . can't find none of his own. He's got to move in on his buddy like . . . you follow me, Marg? (*Pauses. Looks at* MARGY, *at bales*) I mean, don't be flattered none if this one makes a move on you, 'cause it's not that he's likin' you any. (*Pauses*) The fact is, he made some wicked awful remarks just before you came in through the doors, didn't ya, Georgie?

GEORGE: *C'mon, Arch!*

ARCHIE: *Bulllllshit,* buddy! *Bulllllshit!*

GEORGE (*To* MARGY): Here we go.

ARCHIE: First grade. I'm seeing Esther what's'it. Walking her home from school every day. What do you think I find out? (MARGY *stares at* ARCHIE) This one here? He's sending her notes. Notes. He's slipping them to her behind my back. (*Confidentially*) Six to eight of 'em fell outta her reader. (*Pauses, remembering*) "Dick and Jane" and six to eight God damned love letters from old George K. Ferguson. (*Pauses; then angrily*) God damn it, Georgie. *God damn it!*

GEORGE (*to* ARCHIE): This was a resolved matter. This was an incident that was put to bed.

ARCHIE (*to* GEORGE): I'm wakin' it up, George. I'm callin' it right down to breakfast.

MARGY (*calling out*): Excuse meee! (ARCHIE *and* GEORGE *turn to her; their altercation postponed*) Listen, you guys . . . you two should be alone. You two seem . . . busy. I should . . . well . . . *go.*

ARCHIE: What's this?

(MARGIE *goes to locker, gets her coat, pocketbook; moves toward door, pausing only to say her goodbye.* ARCHIE *stands stunned*)

MARGY: It was lovely to see you both again, really, but I do think enough in one lifetime is actually *enough* . . . so, I'll just be moseying along . . .

(ARCHIE *rushes to loading doors, stands and blocks* MARGY'S *exit. He talks to her, plaintively, sincerely*)

ARCHIE: Please stay, Marg. Please don't go. I was so happy to be seein' you like this . . . to be goin' out with you and all. Please . . . don't go. (*Confidentially*) He's not my friend, Marg. Georgie K. Ferguson is no friend of Archie Crisp's. Honest ta God. I'm not like that at all. Don't you worry none. (*To* GEORGE) I'll kill you, George. I swear to God, I'll kill you! Please stay with me. Don't go. *Please?*

MARGY: I don't think so, Archie, really. . . . I mean, well, *why* ?

ARCHIE: Because it's *us*! Because we haven't *talked* . . . we haven't, I dunno, *be'n together yet*! Jesus, Margy, I think about you all the time. I mean, gawd! I've be'n *waitin' and waitin' and waitin'* for tonight, and here it is, and, oh God, please . . . don't go. Stay. You got nothin' to worry about here . . . with us. . . . (*Flashes a look at* GEORGE) It's okay. I swear to you. Please? Stay?

MARGY (*Looking at* ARCHIE. *Pauses. Looks at* GEORGE. *Pauses. Speaks to* ARCHIE, *softly*): Okay, Archie. I'll stay. I'll do that for you.

ARCHIE: That's good. That's great. (*To* GEORGE) She's staying. (*To* MARGY) That's really *so incredibly great*!

(MARGY *hands* ARCHIE *her coat. He is puzzled for a moment, but then realizes that the coat is to be replaced on the hanger. He does this. Turns. smiles at* MARGY, *awkwardly.* ARCHIE *is delighted.*

MARGY *looks about the room, silently. She looks at* GEORGE; *smiles. She look at* ARCHIE; *smiles; speaks.*)

MARGY: What's his "K" for?

ARCHIE: Huh?

MARGY: His "K" . . . you mentioned a "K." I have a vague memory of an extremely nasty little guy with a "K" in the middle. What's it for?

(GEORGE *moans*)

ARCHIE (*giggling*): Tell her.

GEORGE: C'mon, huh, Arch?

ARCHIE: You tell her, or I'll tell her. You got a choice.

GEORGE: Kermit.

MARGY: No kidding?

ARCHIE (*To* GEORGE, *teasing*): Kermie, Kermie . . .

GEORGE: C'mon, Archie . . .

ARCHIE: Kermie, Kermie, Kermie . . .

GEORGE: God damn it, Archie, c'mon . . .

ARCHIE: Kermie, Kermie, Kermie, Kermie . . .

GEORGE (*throwing a punch, while* ARCHIE *sidesteps, laughing*): God damn it, lay off. (*Works at baler*)

ARCHIE (*laughing and pounding his fists against his legs, he moves across the room away from* GEORGE,

wiping his eyes): Whooooeee! I love a laugh!
Whooo . . .

MARGY (*a sudden memory*): Esther *Larkin*: that was the
name of your first grade girlfriend. She lived on the
corner of Prospect and Elm. Pigtails.

ARCHIE: Yup. That's her.

MARGY: Edgar went with Esther Larkin.

ARCHIE: Who's Edgar?

GEORGE: Her *husband*. (*Throws paper into baler*)

ARCHIE: Oh. (*Smiles*) Too much alcohol. Rots the brain.

GEORGE: You can say *that* again!

ARCHIE: They call this one "Chief Hollow Leg" . . .
counta there's no end in sight for the precious
brew . . .

GEORGE: Me. That's a laugh. This one Marg; he's in-
vested his life savings in Tap'a'Keg.

ARCHIE: She don't know what you're talkin' about.

GEORGE (*To* MARGY): Tap'a'Keg's out on Route 1.
You've never been?

MARGY: Yes, George, I must confess: in the matter of
Tap'a'Keg, I have never been.

GEORGE: We could shoot down there one night together, Marg. In your powder blue Studie.

ARCHIE: You makin' another move here?

GEORGE: What da ya mean?

ARCHIE: What do you mean "What da ya mean?" (*Imitates* GEORGE) "We can just shoot down there together, Marg . . . in yo'r powder blue Studie–doo." (*Imitation ceases*) *Bulllllllshit*, buddy! *Bullllshit!* That is a definite move you're makin' on my supper date and I don't like what I'm seein' at *all*! *Not at all*!

GEORGE: This one's seein' moves that aren't bein' made.

ARCHIE (*pulling rank*): Why don't you knock off, George. I can finish up here.

GEORGE (*hurt; defensively*): I'll knock off, but you won't have your bales wired for no uncle by no ha'pahst four in the mornin', and that's a definite *fact* . . . less you're figurin' Margy here's gonna do some of your work for you.

MARGY: I wouldn't mind.

ARCHIE (*laughing*): Woman your size wouldn't get much pressed, Marg.

GEORGE (*laughing as well*): This baler wants beef . . . like me and Arch . . .

ARCHIE: Some of these bales weigh 800 pounds . . .

GEORGE: Minimum . . .

ARCHIE: Takes weight and muscle . . .

GEORGE: Beef . . .

ARCHIE: Be'n doin' this for years . . .

GEORGE: Archie's got a skill.

ARCHIE: This is *man's* work.

GEORGE: Man's work.

MARGY: I wouldn't mind helping.

ARCHIE: Doin' what?

MARGY: Why not?

GEORGE: Why not, Arch?

ARCHIE: Okay, no reason. Work beats just watching, huh?

MARGY: Working certainly does beat just watching, Archie.

GEORGE (*checking out* MARGY's *breasts*): Take your coat–sweater off, Marg . . .

(GEORGE *reaches for her coat–sweater, staring.* ARCHIE *glares at* GEORGE, *staring him down.* MARGY *smiles at each of them; slips out of her coat.*)

GEORGE (*to* ARCHIE; *a child's defense*): I didn't mean anything there . . .

ARCHIE: Here are some gloves. Grab a bundle, toss it on up to Kermit and you're on the clock.

MARGY: We used to have a four–on–the–floor stick shift. Old black DeSoto. Edgar said I'd never be able to press the stick down. It took a lot of weight and muscle. Beef. (*Pauses*) I did it. I took the stick in my hand and I kind of stood over it. All my might . . . I pushed . . . it gave . . . the gears meshed . . . we jerked forward. Burned rubber. (*Pauses*) First to fourth in 15 seconds and that's no bull. We blasted off. Rubber all over the road. (*Pauses*) Women can drive, when they want to. You'd be surprised. (*Moves to* ARCHIE, *turns, beside him; faces baler*) So? How does this thing work?

(ARCHIE *and* GEORGE *are dumbstruck.* ARCHIE *breaks the silence*)

ARCHIE: I take a sizable bundle in my hand and load in from the front for awhile. Then I pull myself up onto the lip and throw down from the top 'til she's ready. . . . Then I start my down–strokes . . . lowering the shaft–head . . . squashing her down. When the belly of the bale's as flat as she's ever gonna' be, I wire her up, tie her off and I'm on to the next one.

MARGY (*after a pause; smiling*): That is . . . impressive, Archie. I am . . . impressed.

(ARCHIE *moves next to* MARGY, *talks to her with some degree of confidence*)

ARCHIE: In what grade did Edgar go with Esther?

MARGY: Edgar and Esther? Go with? Oh, well . . . 9th grade.

ARCHIE: I sure am a blank on your husband, Marg.

MARGY: Edgar wasn't very loud . . . not back then. Not recently, either, I suppose.

GEORGE: Couldn'ta be'n. (MARGY *turns, looks at* GEORGE) Loud. Couldn'ta be'n. I woulda heard him, if he'da made a noise.

ARCHIE (*to* GEORGE): What's the matter with you?

GEORGE: What do you mean?

ARCHIE (*angrily*): What do you *mean*, "What do you mean?" (ARCHIE *moves near bales.* MARGY *counters to look at baler*) This girl is talking about a deceased husband, George. What you've got here is a sympathetic moment and you're talkin' really low class . . . *no* class! (*Pauses*) Sometimes, I'm truly embarrassed to have be'n your friend . . . (*To* MARGY) George Ferguson and I were formerly close friends, Marg. Not for years. (*Pauses; to* GEORGE) When you're a kid you take what's in the neighborhood. You don't think about it: you take it. You were in the neighborhood, so I figured we were friends and hung out with you. I mean, don't flatter yourself none, George. Now that I see you and I'm not a kid . . . well . . . I'm hardly comin' on to you like a friend, right? *You're* the one's runnin' over here to *me* to help . . . not the reverse.

GEORGE: Just what the hell're you sayin', Arch? You wouldn't help me if the chips were down?

ARCHIE (*quickly*): If the chips were down for you, George, I wouldn't be runnin' to you out of friendship. I'd run to you, alright, but it would be out of pity . . . out of feelin' sorry for you, yes, but certainly never . . . not ever . . . out of friendship. (*Pauses*) You understand that? You follow? (*To* MARGY) You see, Marg, sometimes people look the truth straight in the eye, but they see absolutely nothing like what's there. They see sugar where there's salt, that kind of thing.

MARGY (*cutting* ARCHIE *off*): Aren't you getting hungry, Archie?

GEORGE (*whooping as might a large bird*): Whooooaa–a, Archie! Your supper date's gettin' anxious here. Ohoooo–aaahhh oooooo!

ARCHIE: What are you? Soft in the head?

GEORGE: You getting a little hollow in the stomach, Margy?

ARCHIE: You're getting hollow in the head, George!

GEORGE: Munch, munch, hey, Marg?

ARCHIE: What are you? Talking dirty now?

GEORGE: This one can't take a joke at all, Marg.

ARCHIE: I'll bust your squash!

GEORGE (*laughing as he shadowboxes with* ARCHIE):
Got no sense of humor, Archie! You got none!

ARCHIE: This'll put a smile on your face! (ARCHIE *tries to butt* GEORGE *with the top of his head, misses and falls forward against bale.* GEORGE *laughs.* ARCHIE *tries to butt* GEORGE *once again. This time,* GEORGE *sidesteps* ARCHIE, *who races past* GEORGE *and falls on to the dune–like mound of loose newspapers upstage.* GEORGE *whoops with laughter.* ARCHIE *stands, goes to baler and slaps its sides; then he goes to a bale and kicks it*) God damn. God damn. God *damn!* (AR-CHIE *goes to* MARGY, *looks at her.* MARGY *laughs*) What are *you* laughing at?

MARGY: You. Butting your head in the air like a goat.

GEORGE (*thrilled*): A goat, Arch, a goat! She remembers! A goat!

ARCHIE (*to* GEORGE): I'll kill you!

MARGY: You always did that, Arch, even when we were in first grade. You butted your head in the air and made little goat–like noises . . .

(GEORGE *giggles, happily*)

ARCHIE (*to* MARGY): I don't like this.

(ARCHIE *goes to* GEORGE *and slaps him with a fierce backhand*)

GEORGE: Hey, c'mon, Archie, huh?

ARCHIE (*to* MARGY): Every time you make a smart remark that runs me down, I'm gonna hurt your friend
here more. You get me? You follow me?

GEORGE: No more smart remarks, Marg.

MARGY: To which smart remark, precisely, do you re-
fer, Archie?

ARCHIE: Okay. (*Slaps* GEORGE) *That* one. "Precisely."

GEORGE: *Hey, dammit!*

ARCHIE (*holding* GEORGE *in a hammerlock*): I got feelin's here, ya' know.

MARGY: Okay, Archie. No more smart remarks.

ARCHIE: Okay, good. (*Lets loose of* GEORGE) You're free.

GEORGE (*sulking; humiliated; he throws paper into the
baler. He gets a bundle, loads it into baler as well*):
Let's get some work done. I've got a heavy date tonight and I don't wanna be late.

ARCHIE (*laughing*): You got a heavy what?

GEORGE: Let's get some work done, okay?

ARCHIE: No, no. . . . C'mon, Georgie . . . I wanna
hear that again: You've got a heavy *what*?

GEORGE (*quietly*): I said "date."

ARCHIE: Date? Is that dried fruit? Like a fig?

GEORGE: Yuh, dried fruit. Like a fig.

ARCHIE (*to* MARGY): You hear that? George has got to get outta here count of a big fig.

GEORGE: Yuh. Right. You got it, Arch. I've gotta get outta here count of a big fig, so let's get ta packin', okay? (*Turns to* ARCHIE, *squares off*) That okay with you, Arch, if we finish here?

ARCHIE (*giggling*): I thought up a good one! You listening, George? Here it comes. Stay outta the sun, George, 'cause if you stay in the sun too long, you yourself will be . . . a *dried fruit.* (*He whoops and cackles*)

GEORGE: Wicked funny.

ARCHIE: *You get it* ? (*Chuckling and rasping*) You get it, George? A dried fruit! *You get it*??

GEORGE: No, I didn't get it. I'm a Mongolian idiot, so I missed the point. (*Turns away; then back again all of a sudden*) A *course,* I got it, ya goddam goat! What da ya think I am? Thick in the head?? You coulda pulled that one on a wood fence, the fence woulda got it. (*Turns away again, then back*) God damn it, Archie! God damn it! (*Then ever so softly; his feelings are hurt*) God damn it, Archie. God damn it . . .

ARCHIE: What was it you called me? (*Pauses*) Came in between the "Mongolian idiot" and the "wood fence." You remember?

GEORGE: Uh–uh, I don't.

ARCHIE: Starts with a "G" . . .

GEORGE: C'mon, Archie . . .

ARCHIE: That really pisses me off, ya know that?

GEORGE: Don't be dumb, Arch . . .

ARCHIE: Makes me see red . . .

GEORGE: Just 'cause I called you Goat?

ARCHIE: What am I hearing here?

GEORGE: Everybody calls you Goat . . .

ARCHIE: I'll break your back!

GEORGE: Goat's as much your name as Archie is . . .

ARCHIE: I'll rip your pecker off!

GEORGE: Goat is your God damn name!

(ARCHIE *is now choking* GEORGE)

GEORGE: Tell him, Margy! Tell him! Tell him! *Tell him*!

MARGY: It is, Goat.

ARCHIE: I don't like this.

MARGY: Everybody knows you as Goat . . .

ARCHIE (*letting loose of* GEORGE's *throat*): I don't like this at all . . .

MARGY: You've been Goat from the first grade on . . . Arnold . . .

ARCHIE: I never liked Arnold, neither . . .

GEORGE: For God's sakes, uh, Archie . . . Arnold is your God–given name! You were christened Arnold . . . not Goat or Archie . . .

ARCHIE: I've always liked Archie.

GEORGE: I can understand that . . . Archie.

ARCHIE: I'd rather not be called the other. Okay?

GEORGE: Sure. Sure thing . . . Arch. (*Worries*) Is Arch okay? Or do you want the whole thing: Arch*ie*.

ARCHIE: Arch is fine. Arch is fine.

(*Silence*)

MARGY: Edgar hated his name. That's why he picked "Moose."

GEORGE and ARCHIE (*comes the dawn*): Moose!

GEORGE: Moose Burke. Moose, for God's sakes, *Moose*!

ARCHIE: God damn Moose God damn Burke. Old Stiff–antler Moose Burke. How come you didn't say Moose right off the bat? Jez–us, Margy!

GEORGE: Moose Burke. Hot damn. Moose God damn Burke. Hot God damn *damn!*

ARCHIE: I remember Moose Burke when he was four. . . . No! Three! Little Moosie Burke! (*Cackles*) Moosie Burke. Little Stiff–antler Moosie . . .

GEORGE: I remember Moose when he could run the hundred in ten–two . . .

MARGY: That wasn't Edgar . . .

ARCHIE: That wasn't Moose?

GEORGE: What are you? Kiddin' me?

MARGY: That wasn't him at all.

ARCHIE: No . . . That was Artie What's'it . . . the Jew. He won Longest–Distance–Traveled two/three times . . . skinny . . .

GEORGE: Artie? Yuh. I think so. (*Pauses*) So who the fuck is Moose? (*Embarrassed*) Pardon me, Marg, huh? My mouth, huh?

ARCHIE: Outta control . . . like a freight train, huh? Say you're sorry to the lady, huh, George.

MARGY: I don't mind, really. Really, I don't mind . . .

ARCHIE: Let's *hear* it, toilet!

GEORGE: I said I'm sorry, Arch. (ARCHIE *glares at* GEORGE) Okay, okay. I'm sorry, Marg . . . I am.

MARGY: There's no need.

ARCHIE: There's need.

MARGY: There's no need. None.

ARCHIE: You mean that, or are you just bein' nice?

MARGY (*suddenly angry*): I said there was no need. (*She snaps at them*) I said there was no need. Didn't you hear me?

ARCHIE (*after an embarrassed moment*): Okay, okay. (*To* GEORGE). Take it back, George.

GEORGE: Huh?

ARCHIE: No need. The lady says no need. Take it back.

GEORGE: You mean the apology? (ARCHIE *nods;* GEORGE *stares*) You mean I should take back the apology? (ARCHIE *nods again*) This is dumb. (ARCHIE *glares*) You mean like, "I'm not sorry"? . . . (ARCHIE *nods;* GEORGE *turns to* MARGY, *smiles.*) I'm not sorry, Margy. (GEORGE *giggles*) This is truly dumb . . . (*Pauses, straightfaced*) I am not at all sorry, Marg . . . (*Giggles*) I said what I said . . . (*Pauses; thinks*) What'd I say? Oh, yuh. Oh, yuh. I'm not sorry I asked who the fuck Moose was. . . .

(*He laughs, looks at glaring* ARCHIE, *who looks at smiling* MARGY *and shrugs to* GEORGE, *who shrugs back to* ARCHIE *and giggles*)

MARGY (*Looking at watch*) We should think about supper, hmm?

GEORGE: Me?

ARCHIE: Not him.

GEORGE: Not me: Archie, Marg.

ARCHIE: Not him: I'm the one you called for supper, not George.

MARGY: I didn't know George would be with us. George is one of the old gang, right, Archie? We're all in this together, right? All–for–one–one–for–all kinda thing, right?

GEORGE: Now, that is real nice of you, Marg.

ARCHIE: I don't like this.

GEORGE: I couldn't accept. (*To* ARCHIE) I didn't accept.

ARCHIE: He already has a date. You heard him.

GEORGE: True. True. I do. I do.

MARGY: With whom?

GEORGE: Who?

MARGY: With whom?

ARCHIE: With a fig.

MARGY: With whom, Georgie? Somebody we know? Somebody who might have been a cheerleader? A twirler? A top speller? A class clown? A most–likely–to–succeed? With whom, Georgie, whom? (*Pauses; moves to* GEORGE) I am really quite curious, George. Really amazingly so . . . strikingly so . . . I should even say remarkably so. (*Pauses; waits a moment, staring at the astonished* GEORGE; *then, with a strong, studied Boston accent, she again speaks*) I'm wicked awful anxious for yo'r answer, George! Let's hear it!

GEORGE (*stunned*): What . . . what are you . . . askin'?

MARGY: Who's your date, George? Who's the lucky . . . piece of fruit?

GEORGE: I . . . I don't have any, Margy.

MARGY: Any what, George? The antecedent to your pronoun is somehow quite obscure. Any date? Any fruit? Any what, George, hmmm?

GEORGE: Any date. I got no date.

MARGY: A good–looking fellow like you? No date? What is this world coming to? (*Pauses*) There's a Chinese take–out on Route 28, George, down by the miniature golf. You have money?

GEORGE: Well, yuh . . . for what?

MARGY: Moo shoo pork and three pancakes . . .

ARCHIE: What's going on here?

MARGY: George is going out for food . . . for the three of us.

GEORGE: I'm not that hungry . . .

ARCHIE: You and I are going out alone, Margy. That's a deal.

MARGY: George is going out, Archie. Right now. You and I are staying here . . . alone.

GEORGE: What are you? Planning som'pin' while I'm gone, Margy?

MARGY: In what sense, George?

GEORGE: With Archie?

MARGY: Am I planning som'pin'? With Archie? While you're gone, George? (*Pauses*) Such as what?

GEORGE: Oh, I dunno . . . hanky–panky . . .

MARGY: Am I planning hanky–panky with Archie while you're gone, George? Maybe I am.

(MARGY *walks, wordlessly, around* ARCHIE. *She now stands behind* ARCHIE, *who looks at* MARGY *as though she's just agreed to* "hanky–panky" . . . *and then some*)

ARCHIE: Write down our orders, George.

GEORGE: I don't like this.

ARCHIE (*taking pencil and paper*): You write 'em out, Margy, so's George can just give 'em over to the Chinaman . . . okay?

MARGY (*with a thick Boston accent*): Sure. (*She takes pad and pencil*) My husband, Edgar, was an absolute fiend for the Oriental . . . especially moo shoo pork. He loved to roll his own . . .

GEORGE: How come you like Archie, Marg? How come you picked him, say, over me?

ARCHIE: What's this I'm hearing?

GEORGE: I'm just curious, Arch! No sweat! No sweat here at all, huh? No *suh*!

MARGY: Picked Archie, George? How come? You mean over all the guys in our little gang?

GEORGE: Well, over, say, *me*, yuh.

MARGY: Picked Archie over you, ohhh . . . well, for one thing, George, I forgot you altogether. Nothing personal in it, mind you, but you'd just melted into the faceless pack. You were specifically forgotten, George. In fact, to this very moment, the best I can do is come up with a very porky, very mean little guy with a middle "K" like yours, but that couldn't've be'n you, right? (*Smiles, shrugs*) As for "picking" Archie, we bumped into each other at Mal's. I smiled, he smiled. I called him for dinner, he accepted. And that is the long and short of it, George. I am getting quite hungry. I would hate to return to my poor brother's deathbed unfed. It's a tough enough vigil, as it is. Don't you agree? (*Suddenly angry*) Don't . . . you . . . agree?

GEORGE (*after a confused pause*): Yeah, well, I lost a lot a weight right after senior year. Yuh . . . I did.

MARGY (*getting her sweater, starting upstage*): Listen, you guys, I'll go off for dinner, okay? You keep working . . . you stay put. I'll go.

ARCHIE: Like hell you will! (*To* GEORGE) Like hell she will . . . huh?

GEORGE: I'll do it.

ARCHIE: Right. (ARCHIE *shoves* GEORGE *toward door*)

MARGY: Nonsense . . . I wouldn't want to split you two up . . .

GEORGE: No, I'll do it . . .

(ARCHIE *throws* GEORGE'*s jacket at him*)

ARCHIE: Go, George!

GEORGE: I said I would. (*Starts toward loading door*) I don't know where. (*To* MARGY) Where?

MARGY: Chinese take–out. Route 28, Stoneham. Is it still there? (*Writes out order*)

ARCHIE: Yup. Chinese place, near the miniature golf . . .

MARGY: Here, George. Hand this note to the Chinese man at the counter, and, for God's sake, tip him fifteen percent! Go now, go, go . . . shoo . . . scat . . .

ARCHIE: You heard her!

GEORGE (*starting toward loading door, he stops*): I really hate this . . . (*Starts again and stops*) A nice girl like you, Margy. Swede'd be pissed . . .

ARCHIE: Will you get movin'? We're famished here! We want some grub, huh? You're keepin' us from it. George! That ain't nice or polite!

GEORGE: That's just bullshit! You're just tryin' ta get alone with Margy.

ARCHIE: I'll kill you, George. I swear ta God I will!

MARGY: Go, George . . . (*Smiles*) It's alright . . . (*Pauses*) Really . . .

GEORGE (*moving to door; stops*): I'm gonna make this real fast. Don't you worry . . .

(GEORGE *exits.* ARCHIE *looks at* MARGY *and smiles. He moves to the loading doors, closes them*)

ARCHIE: Well, huh, well, look at us, huh, Marg . . . just the two of us, huh? All alone here . . . you and me.

Wellllll . . . (*Smiles. There is a short silence*) How's it goin'?

MARGY: It's going quite well, Archie. Quite well. I'm so glad to be back . . . to have seen you again . . . and George . . . in the flesh . . . (*Smiles, pauses. There is a short silence*) We've got our work cut out for us, don't we, Arch?

ARCHIE (*motioning to baler*): This? (MARGY *laughs*) You mean baling? (MARGY *stares at* ARCHIE, *who shifts his weight nervously from foot to foot*) Uh, Marg, if we're gonna . . . you know . . . we'd, uh, better, uh, well, uh, you know, right?

MARGY: I beg your pardon?

ARCHIE: Uh, well, there isn't a lot of time, Marg . . .

MARGY: For what purpose? (ARCHIE *walks to her, wordlessly, embarrassed. He puckers up his lips and waits to be kissed; his lips and face on the open air between them.* MARGY *stares at him a moment; smiles*) Oh, I see: kissing?

ARCHIE: Do you . . . wanna?

MARGY: Oh, well, no, Archie, I don't wanna . . . really. I think you and I have done enough kissing for one lifetime, don't you, Archie, really?

ARCHIE: I, uh, I can understand 'n all . . . really, sure. Yuh, well, I do, yuh, I do understand. (*Pauses*) I'm a *lunk*, right? A real lunk . . .

MARGY: No, Archie . . . that's hardly the reason . . .

ARCHIE: That's the reason. It's true, too. I'm a lunk . . . a local . . . a lummox, too. I understand, I do, yuh, I do understand. You went away and you got yourself *terrific* . . . really . . . ya did, Marg. You look just *great*! Here I am: Archie Crisp. I mean, Christ! What've I got to offer a woman's traveled halfway around the world, probably? Maybe even all the way . . .

MARGY: All the way. Yuh. Twice.

ARCHIE: Ya see?? Twice. Jees, Marg, don't let it worry ya none, really. You don't wanna make love with old Archie Crisp, he's gonna understand, really. Call me crazy, Marg, but I really do understand. Really, I know that. I do, uh, well, I do kinda hav'ta ask a favor of you, though, Marg, if ya don't mind . . .

MARGY: What's the favor, Archie?

ARCHIE: I agree to your stipulation of no lovemakin' and hands–off and all, but Marg? . . . this is really important to me. . . . (*He pauses; looks down and then to her directly*) Don't tell George, okay?

(MARGY *turns from* ARCHIE, *smiles. She pauses a moment. Her smile is gone. She faces* ARCHIE *again*)

MARGY: I was seventeen, Archie. Seventeen . . .

(ARCHIE *averts his eyes; faces front, bows his head*)

End of Act One

ACT II

Later, same night.

Lights up. If Act I lighting was, in part, daylight through shop's skylights, Act II's lighting is totally from electrical fixtures, overhead.

GEORGE *sits on chair stage right, drinking beer, watching* ARCHIE *and* MARGY *sit on bale, upstage of* GEORGE, *finishing meal; rapt attention paid to* ARCHIE, *who performs the story now for* MARGY, *enthusiastically.*

GEORGE *watches, jealous of* ARCHIE'S *attention to* MARGY, *and, at the same time, jealous of* MARGY'S *attention to* ARCHIE.

Remains of GEORGE *and* ARCHIE'S *eaten Chinese take-out meals visible. Many crushed beer cans (dead soldiers) near* GEORGE'S *feet*

ARCHIE: When I was a little guy, I used to work here every Saturday. I got two bucks, which was a big deal then . . . wicked big. (*Smiles*) Used ta be maybe seven, eight winos used ta work here weekends . . . for my Uncle Max. . . . I was just a kid. (*Pauses; lost in a memory*) "Lum" is what we called the big one. His name was Alfred, I think . . . some people called him Allie. Most of us called him "Lumbago" on accounta he had it. For short, we called him "Lum." Dumbest, meanest son–of–a–bitch ten towns around, and that's a fact. (*Pauses*) My particular specialty was to climb into the baler, counta I was a kid and little and all, and push the newspapers tight into the corners. A good bale has sharp edges. The only thing was, getting inside the press spooked me. Gave me the willies. (*Pauses*) Lum always used to threaten me when I was in here. He used ta say he'd pull the top over me when I was inside. Then he'd say they'd press me in with the overissues and sell me in the bale and I'd get driven up to Fitchburg to Felulah's Mill, and I'd get dumped into the acid bath with the overissues and come outta the wet press up there, rolled into fine paper for stationery. (*Pauses*) The miserable son–of–a–bitch! Tellin' that to a kid, huh? He grabbed me in a headlock one Saturday, right here on this spot. Lum. No warning at all. He just grabbed me. I figured I was a dead kid, ya know. I mean, I was eleven and he was forty. The odds weren't exactly on *me*, ya know what I mean? But, I took a major shot and I whipped him around backwards. (*He looks at* GEORGE, *who averts his eyes*) I ran myself forward as fast as I could, whipping him around backwards . . . and he flew! He *flew*! He hit the front of the baler so hard, it was like his face exploded. He landed on the stack and just lay there, blood oozing out of him, staining the papers. (*Pauses*) I figured I'd killed him. (*Pauses*) Winos grumblin', lookin' this way and that. . . . They started fadin' outta the shop . . . the winos. (*Pauses*) I was scared shit. Just me alone and the body: Lum. (*Pauses*) I figured the cops would give me the electric chair . . . or worse; hangin'. (*Pauses*) I was scared shit. (*Pauses*) I figured the only way was to get rid of the body, hide him. The winos wouldn't talk. Nobody'd miss him, anyway, right? (*Pauses*) So, I started draggin' him over to the baler . . . to throw him in. I was only eleven, Marg. Can you get the picture? (ARCHIE *moves to baler to better illustrate his story.* GEORGE *will soon move in closer to* MARGY *and this time,* ARCHIE *will register jealousy. Without a break in his storytelling,* ARCHIE *will shove* GEORGE *aside and complete his story)* Me, eleven, draggin' this forty–year–old drunken corpse by the arm to the press here *(Pauses)* This very one . . . *(Slaps baler, pauses, smiles)* You'll never guess what happened, Marg. You'll never in a million years guess . . . *(Laughs)* Gave me bad dreams for about eighteen years. *(Pauses)* Lum got up. I swear to God. He opens his eyes . . . blinks som'pin' wicked . . . and then . . . then . . . *(Laughs)* Lum gets up, as though from the dead. The cut wasn't that deep. He musta been out as much from the wine as from the hitting the baler. *(Pauses)* I figured he was gonna kill me, Margy. Get even. He didn't. He shook his head a couple of times . . . moves to his chino Eisenhower jacket, and he goes away. No pay. No finishin' the day. No attempt whatsoever to do damage to me. *(Pauses)* That was a big day in the life of this little Arnold "Billy–Goat" Crisp. I can tell you that. *(Pauses)* Gaining respect is what life is all about.

GEORGE *(from the chair)*: Lum ever come back?

ARCHIE: Huh?

GEORGE: Lum ever come back here? To work? To talk to you? Whatever?

ARCHIE: What the hell kind of question is that?

GEORGE: It's a question. It's a question.

(GEORGE *stands, tosses food container and beer can into trash, walks around back of baler, arrives between* MARGY *and* ARCHIE)

ARCHIE: You mean, did Lum ever come back here to *get* me? Is that what you mean?

GEORGE: I didn't mean that exactly. I meant, maybe, to work again, to just *be* . . . around here and all. Did you ever have to look him in the eye? Face to face. Did he ever . . . well . . . yuh . . . I suppose . . . try to get you.

ARCHIE: Once, yuh, he did once.

GEORGE: When?

ARCHIE: I'm done talkin' on this subject.

(ARCHIE *slams down his packet of newspaper on to the floor instead of into the baler and storms off away from* GEORGE *and* MARGY. *He exits through loading doors, slamming door as he goes*)

MARGY: What was that about, George?

GEORGE: He's still jealous.

MARGY: Of what?

GEORGE: Not what: *who.*

MARGY: Of who? (*Corrects herself*) Of *whom.* (*Smiles*) Sorry, George, but I've never been comfortable treating an objective pronoun like a nominative pronoun. I'm sure you understand my meticulousness. I do hope you forgive me.

GEORGE: How come you pretend like you're not a schoolteacher? Everybody knows that you are.

MARGY: But I'm not.

GEORGE: But you are. It's a fact. Everybody knows . . .

MARGY: I work for a college, but I don't actually teach.

GEORGE: New York University?

MARGY: Well, yes. How did you know that:

GEORGE: Lucky guess. What do you do if you don't teach?

MARGY: What do I do? (*Smiles*) I criticize.

GEORGE: Really.

MARGY: Yup. Really.

GEORGE: What?

MARGY: What do I criticize? What other people write.

GEORGE: You mean like "good" or "bad" sorta thing?

MARGY: Approximately that, yuh.

GEORGE: Don't people get like *annoyed*?

MARGY: The people I criticize? Uh, well, sometimes, yes.

GEORGE: You get *paid* for that?

MARGY: I do. Yes.

GEORGE: Must be nice.

MARGY: Being paid to criticize? Nice? This is *exhausting*! (*Smiles*) What do you do?

GEORGE: For money?

MARGY: Yuh. For money.

GEORGE: I, uh, well, usual thing.

MARGY: Really?

GEORGE: Yuh, well . . . yuh.

MARGY: What, uh, uh, what would that be, George: "the usual thing"?

GEORGE: I'm, uh, on the Town . . .

(*He looks about nervously to see if* ARCHIE *has heard him*)

MARGY: On the Town?

GEORGE (*quietly*): Yuh, well . . . yuh. I've be'n doin' it straight through since high school and all: on the Town. (*Pauses*) It's a steady thing, ya know. Not too

exciting, maybe. I mean, not som'pin' like what yo're
use'ta, for example, but, it's who I am and what I do
. . . as far as money goes kinda thing . . .

MARGY: You're "on the Town" for money? There was a
musical comedy by that name. You're not telling me
you sing and dance *professionally,* are you, George?

GEORGE: I'm on the Town crew.

MARGY: Oh . . .

GEORGE: Cleanin', sweepin', shovelin' sort a thing.
Whatever's needed, kinda. . . . I had longevity on
the Gulch crew . . . ya remember? Guinea Gulch?

MARGY: Oh. Right. Italians . . . Water Street . . .
Guinea Gulch . . . I'd forgotten that.

GEORGE: I was top dog on the Gulch crew for ten years.
Seniority, that sorta thing. (*Suddenly*) They laid me
off. Just before last Christmas. God damn town was
near broke. They laid me off and Porker Watson—
'member him?—and Stoney Webster: the rotten
three of us. Merry Christmas, huh? The whole God
damn town was very nearly bankrupt. (*Pauses*) I
don't care. I don't. I mean, who wants ta spend their
life cleaning up Guinea Gulch, right? It's great when
yo'r a high school kid, pullin' down maybe sixty–five a
week. Hey, that's big bucks, right? But when yo're
thirty–seven, goin' on thirty–eight, Marg, and they're
still payin' ya the minimum wage, huh?

MARGY: You haven't worked since last Christmas?

GEORGE: A year ago last Christmas. No. Nothin'. Things are slim around these parts, Marg. It ain't the good old days, huh? (*Smiles*) Hell, I ain't kickin' none . . . give me a chance ta think. All them years, sitting on trucks with six/seven/eight other guys. No time to think. Always laughin' and kiddin' around . . . drinkin' beers 'n all . . . acting like juveniles, really. It was a wicked awful waste a my time. I'm glad . . . (*Quietly*) Buncha' blow'ahs. (*Pauses a moment; then to* MARGY, *smiles*) In the days when you and I were . . . ya know . . . intimately friends kinda . . . well . . . ya know . . . money was easy . . . I mean, what did it take, huh? A couple of bucks for this or that? Pizzas, dancin', maybe a tank of gas? *Shit!* Easy as fallin' off a log!

MARGY: When, George?

GEORGE: When what?

MARGY: When did I know you?

GEORGE: All our lives.

MARGY: Intimately. When intimately? When exactly were we "intimately friends kinda"?

GEORGE: You've got to be kidding, Marg.

MARGY: I'm not, Georgie, I'm not. I don't mean to hurt your feelings, but I remember your name and that is, as they say, just about *it.*

GEORGE: H.M. Warren School, second grade, Georgie Ferguson. Look at me.

MARGY: Georgie Ferguson? Georgie Ferguson? Georgie Kermit Ferguson . . . Kermie . . . Kermie . . . Kermit . . . Georgie Kermie . . . G.K. . . . (*She looks up, hopelessly*) A blank. I am shocked and amazed to announce a blank. (*She smiles*) You made no impression on me at all, George. Not any. None.

GEORGE: Georgie Ferguson. Look at me.

MARGY (*angrily*) *I'm . . . looking . . . at . . . you* !

(*A short silence;* ARCHIE's *voice breaks into the void, from way offstage*)

ARCHIE: He walked you home and sent you notes.

MARGY (*Looking about, amazed.* ARCHIE *cannot be seen. She smiles at* GEORGE): Sorry, but, I believe my silver fillings are picking up police calls.

(ARCHIE *enters, hops up on back edge of baler; repeats his announcement, flatly*)

ARCHIE: He walked you home and sent you notes.

GEORGE (*yelling up to* ARCHIE): Don't start in, Archie. That was a long time ago.

MARGY (*also up to* ARCHIE): Me or Esther?

ARCHIE (*yelling down*): You!

GEORGE: You, too. (*He pretends to be ashamed*) I kinda had a knack with girls, I guess.

MARGY: George, is the implication here that you and I used to . . . *go together?* (GEORGE *nods*) We *went* together? (GEORGE *nods again*) Like a couple? Like "Let's double with George and Margy Saturday night," huh? (*Pauses*) A couple? George and Margy, Margy and George? That kinda thing? (GEORGE *nods*) My God, I don't remember them at all.

GEORGE: I bought you a ball–point . . . at Mrs. Card's store.

MARGY: No kidding?

GEORGE: No kidding.

MARGY: I use a fountain pen now, George. The world has changed. Didn't you hear?

GEORGE: You let me look down your blouse.

MARGY: Down my blouse? In second grade? (GEORGE *nods*) In second grade you looked down my *blouse* . . . at my second grade breasts? (GEORGE *nods again*) The world hasn't changed much in some sectors, has it, Georgie?

(GEORGE *shrugs*)

ARCHIE (*roaring*): If this ain't the most God damn *disgusting display of smut* I ever heard!

(ARCHIE *moves to* MARGY; *pointing his finger in the accusatory. He is attempting to control his anger, which is a considerable effort*)

ARCHIE: I got feelin's, ya know! I got 'em!

MARGY: I beg your pardon?

ARCHIE: I was hiding back there the whole time . . .
listening in. I heard every God damn thing the both
of yous said! Didn't you know that?

MARGY: I had suspicions, yes.

ARCHIE: You knew that?

MARGY: I did, yes.

ARCHIE: A man doesn't hide unless he wants someone
to come looking for him, right?

MARGY: I am simply amazed to hear your . . . incisive-
ness, your trenchance, Archie. I agree. I definitely
agree. I am . . . in agreement.

ARCHIE (*a hostile imitation*): Well, I am simply amazed
to hear that you agree, dearie.

GEORGE: Cool yourself down, Arch . . . c'mon.

ARCHIE: I'll cool yo'r ass!

GEORGE: Come on, Archie!

ARCHIE: You were lookin' down her blouse?

GEORGE: *Every*body was!

ARCHIE: Bullshit!

GEORGE: *Bullshit* to *you!* Everybody was, and you know it *full well!*

MARGY: Could I chime in here?

ARCHIE: Stay outta this!

MARGY: But it's my blouse!

GEORGE: You listen to me, Billy–Goat Crisp, you got no right bringing up no dead issues, some twenty–five/ thirty years after the fact, ya know what I mean? *Do ya?* (*Angrily*) *God damn it!*

ARCHIE: Look at him, why don't ya? Ashamed, right? Isn't he ashamed? Isn't that the look of ashamed that's written all over the son–of–a–bitch?

GEORGE: *Up yours, I'm "ashamed"!* . . . that'll be some cold day in hell when you catch Kermie Ferguson "ashamed"! . . . and that's the God's–honest!

ARCHIE: As for you, sister, you got no shame! No shame! It's one thing for me to be coppin' a look: We were boyfriend and girlfriend and that is a fact. But for this Kermie Ferguson son–of–a–bitchin' bastard? No shame. Nooo . . . shame . . .

MARGY: Could we just hold here a minute?

ARCHIE: You start out dirty, you end up dirty. That's a fact.

MARGY: Could you close it down, please, Archie?

ARCHIE: Showin' your tits around in second grade and look at you now. Look at you now. Some filthy mouth, huh? And where did it start? H.M. Warren School, by the snow fence, second recess. That's where. And I'll tell you another thing . . .

(MARGY *slaps* ARCHIE's *face. There is a stunned silence.* GEORGE *giggles a high–pitched giggle, covering his mouth, feminine, childlike*)

MARGY: Put a belt on that indecorous and milk–curdling giggle of yours, George. I find it far too girlish for our particular circumstance.

GEORGE: *What*??

MARGY: Better. (*To* ARCHIE) First off, the matter of my mammary glands . . . my breasts . . . my *tits* . . . my *boobs* . . . my *jugs* . . . my *knockers* . . . my *set* . . . my *melons* . . . my *funny valentines* . . . my *knobs* . . . (*Smiles*) My *perfect little orbs.* (*Pauses*) They seem to be causing you some grief, my breasts. They've been quite something for me, too, over the years. I can't say I find them quite as . . . exciting as you two do. . . . Lucky for me. Imagine if I were caught up in the irresistibility of my own breasts. Trying to brush my teeth, for example. I would fumble with tube and brush, unable to keep my hands from my fabulous *poitrine*. My teeth would green and decay: rot. . . . Dressing: It would never happen. I'd just keep ripping my shirt away for another look . . . another peek . . . the cop of another feel. First, a bad cold, then pneumonia, then pleurisy . . . dread disease after dread disease . . . ending, no doubt, in death. (*Pauses*) "What a pity she

had breasts, poor thing. They did her in." (*Pauses*)
Thinking it over, Archie and George, I will gladly
give my breasts over to you, for whatever purpose
you choose. George, you would wear them on the
odd days; Archie, on the evens. And I'll be free to get
back to work . . . to get back to sleep at night . . .
to end the constant and unrelenting fondling.
(*Pauses*) I want you to have my breasts, guys. I really
do. You do so seem to envy them.

(*She begins to unbutton her blouse—two buttons only
—to show her breasts to the men upstage*)

ARCHIE: What are you doin'?

GEORGE: What's a matter with you?

MARGY: You should look them over before you agree.
It's a commitment, having breasts like these two
beauties. You should have a look . . . in case you
want to divvy them up, for example. I'm told they're
not quite symmetrical. You might find one to be
somewhat more exciting than the other . . .

GEORGE: Close your shirt . . . (*He looks away; as does*
ARCHIE) Close it.

ARCHIE: You heard him.

MARGY: You sure?

ARCHIE: Close it up.

GEORGE: You sure are weird, Margy . . .

MARGY: You think so? Every time I've been in the right
circumstances for comparison . . . you know . . .
ladies' locker rooms . . . faculty physicals for group
insurance . . . and other orgy–like nude gatherings
of mine, the weaker sex . . . I've, well, compared.
(*Smiles at* GEORGE) I never found mine to be weird,
George. Small, yes, but never weird.

GEORGE: I didn't mean your chest. I meant your attitude.

MARGY: Oh. My attitude. I see. Well, I'll just have to
watch my mental step, won't I? (*Smiles*) I do certainly
beg your pardon, George. I do certainly. (*Fingers buttons on blouse*) Last chance, guys.

GEORGE: Button it up, Marg! You're makin' a fool of
yourself!

MARGY: Archie? Peeks?

ARCHIE: Button it up!

MARGY (*buttoning her blouse*): Thirty years of laser–
beam stares and innuendoes until finally I relinquish
my greedy hold on the adored knockers and *my God!
My God!* (*Imitates* GEORGE) "Button it up, Marg.
You're makin' a fool of yourself." (*Completes buttoning*) There is much I would like to make of myself in
the few spots of time left to make anything at all,
George, but a fool, I must admit, is not on my list.
(*Smiles*) We've settled the breast question, yes? (*No
reply. She asks again.*) George? (*No reply*) Archie?
(GEORGE *and* ARCHIE *turn away*) Now, then . . .
the matter of Archie's saying, "You and I were boy-

friend and girlfriend," meaning, I suppose, you/Archie and I/Margy Palumbo. Is that a fact?

ARCHIE: What are you: cute or som'pin'?

MARGY: Me? Cute? Never!

ARCHIE: We were! Boyfriend and girlfriend.

MARGY: B.F. and G.F.?

ARCHIE: Yuh.

MARGY: Before tonight?

ARCHIE: You oughta have your memory checked.

MARGY: *I* oughta?

GEORGE: Archie's still smartin' 'cause you two were . . . ya know . . . sweethearts, you might say, and I split you up.

ARCHIE: Bullshit, buddy! *Bullshit!* You didn't split nothin' but the supper bill for your last date . . .

GEORGE: What's that s'pose ta mean? You callin' me *cheap?*

ARCHIE: Cheap? You: cheap? That's a laugh! I wouldn't call you just cheap. Callin' you "just cheap" would be like callin' the Pope "just Catholic." You are more than cheap, pally–pal: You are cheap*est.*

MARGY: I don't think you mean "cheap*est*", Archie. I think you mean "cheap*err*." When comparing two cheapskates, one is cheap and the other is cheap*er*. Only when comparison is made among three or more cheapskates does one find the cheap*est*. It's a small point, I know, but *c'est la guerre de la lange Anglais*!

ARCHIE (*to* MARGY): I think we've both had enough smart remarks from you, Margy Palumbo. (*To* GEORGE) Right?

GEORGE: Right! Enough insults . . .

ARCHIE: Highfalutin airs . . .

GEORGE: Hoity–toity airs . . .

ARCHIE: College–girl bullshit . . .

GEORGE: You're really tryin' ta start trouble here . . .

ARCHIE: Between me and George . . .

GEORGE: Me and Archie . . .

ARCHIE: Split us up . . .

GEORGE: Yuh. That's it.

MARGY: Bullll*shit*, buddy!

ARCHIE: This is what you went to college for? To learn how to talk filthy?

GEORGE: Swede should be ashamed.

ARCHIE: She should be ashamed! It's disgusting. Honest to God . . . disgusting!

GEORGE: Great guy, Swede.

ARCHIE: I never liked Swede. I never liked *any* handicapped kids too much, frankly. I've got enough problems of my own. You, leadin' him around like you were some sorta *saint*! All the kids pamperin' the two of yous . . . pretending he was normal and all . . . makin' him Class President and crap like that. "Peter Palumbo For President 'Cause He'll Get The Job Done." I never heard such crap, really! (*To* GEORGE) Where the hell do you come off sayin' you like him? Huh? You never liked Swede Palumbo. You hated him!! Where the Christ do you come off makin' statements like that?

GEORGE: Just makin' conversation. Passin' the day. It's only right.

ARCHIE (*imitating* GEORGE): "Only right." (*To* MARGY) You shoulda heard what he was sayin' before you came in here. He "likes" Swede . . . hah? What crap. You *remember* what Kermie Ferguson did ta Swede? Do ya?

GEORGE: C'mon, Arch, huh?

ARCHIE: Bullshit, buddy. Bullshit. You don't go shovin' him inta line . . . shovin' him hard and then come up with, "I liiike Sweedie–deedie!" Bullllllshit . . .

(*There is a sharp intake of breath from* GEORGE *and* MARGY: *shocked*)

GEORGE: I can't fuckin' believe you just said what you just fuckin' said! I've be'n watchin' my tongue the whole night! Honest ta Christ! (*Laughs*) Makes me *laugh.* (*Roars*) Makes me fuckin' laugh! Call me crazy, Margy, but this just makes me laugh!

MARGY: Call you crazy? Nawww. I'd never call you crazy, George. If you're crazy, then what am I? Then what is Archie? (*Pauses, very upset*) If I were large enough . . . physically . . . I would probably beat you. I would probably try to kill you. If I were large enough . . . physically . . . I would probably try to kill you and I would probably succeed. (*Pauses*) But I would never call you crazy, George. (*Pauses. Attacks* GEORGE, *punches him in a rage. They move onto dune–like mound of papers*) If you aren't the most odious son–of–a–bitch I ever laid eyes on. (*She weeps a moment; punches her fist into her own thigh twice in self–disgust*) Stop crying! Stop crying!

(*She continues to weep. There is a pause.* MARGY's *attitude will change here. She has lost ground. The men will be, for the moment, stronger, more confident than they have been of late.* GEORGE *is the first to speak*)

GEORGE: Look at her. Cryin' . . . weepin' . . . sheddin' tears . . . poor kid.

ARCHIE: God damn. I've hurt her feelings. I feel awful. (*To* MARGY) Shushh, huh. C'mon now, Marg. I'm feelin' just terrible that I made you cry. Come on, huh?

GEORGE: Guys like us, Marg, we don't mean half the things we say. We're just talkin', ya know? Tryin' ta be cool, calm and collected, ya know? (*Moves close to her. She continues to weep*)

ARCHIE: All kiddin' around straight ta hell, Marg, you want a shoulder ta lean on, kinda, you know you've got mine . . . Georgie's, too. I mean, we're, well . . . your pals.

GEORGE: Not just boys on the prowl . . .

ARCHIE: Nothin' like that . . .

GEORGE: We're shootin' straight with you now . . .

ARCHIE: I always liked you, Marg. And that's a fact.

GEORGE: He did. I can vouch for that. I remember.

ARCHIE: You liked her, too.

GEORGE: I did. I did. That's a fact. I did.

ARCHIE: Why are you crying?

GEORGE: She's unhappy.

ARCHIE: What's makin' you unhappy? What, specifically, Margy?

GEORGE: Us, definitely. What we said . . .

ARCHIE: About what? (GEORGE *shrugs*) About what? (ARCHIE *moves close to* MARGY) About what, Margy, about what? I said something about what?

(MARGY *continues to weep*)

GEORGE: I think it was probably me. (*To* MARGY) Was it, Marg? Was it something I said? God damn, I'm really sorry. I hope that you believe me, huh, Marg? I'm really sorry . . . I hate when a woman cries . . .

(MARGY *sneezes into handkerchief. She moves away from the men, but they follow after her, crowding her, forcing her finally against the baler. She will stay there a moment, regain composure, her crying will cease. Her strength will return*)

ARCHIE: Most annoying fuckin' thing in the world!

GEORGE: Drives me crazy . . .

ARCHIE: Drives me nuts . . .

GEORGE: Makes me wanna take right the fuck off!

ARCHIE: Get outta the house! Drive away . . .

GEORGE: *Move* away!

ARCHIE: Make a fist. (*Pauses*) Hit . . . (*Hits his own chest*) Hit . . . (*Again*) Make a fist and hit . . .

(MARGY *moves to* ARCHIE, *places her hand on his cheek. There is a short silence.* ARCHIE *stops raving, settles into her touch, instantly and absolutely calmed.*

GEORGE *is wide-eyed, staring, left out*)

GEORGE: Hey, Marg . . . Arch? Cut the kiddin' around, huh? (*The touch continues*) Come on, you guys . . . (*A false laugh wanted here*)

ARCHIE (*short of breath; quietly*): Ever since second grade, Margy . . . you were the only one. Honest to God . . . (MARGY *turns from* ARCHIE; *faces* GEORGE, *moves to him. He is frightened. She places her hand on* GEORGE's *cheek. She groans, pained to feel* GEORGE's *cheek. He giggles, pulls back from her touch. He places his hand on her cheek.* MARGY *doesn't resist. She moans, pained, somewhat slumped into* GEORGE's *hand*) What gives?

GEORGE: A touch! Just a touch! We were friends, too, ya' know!

ARCHIE: Let loose, George . . .

GEORGE: Come on, Arch . . .

ARCHIE: Drop your hand.

GEORGE: Jesus, Arch . . . you got some kind of sharing problem, or what?

ARCHIE: Drop it, Georgie Ferguson, or I'll mop this place up with you.

GEORGE (*stepping back from* MARGY): Okay? Okay?

ARCHIE (*quietly. His feelings have been somehow hurt*): God damn, Georgie . . . God damn. (*Pauses, turns away*) God damn . . . (ARCHIE *is weeping. He turns*

his face away from GEORGE, *who stares incredu-
lously at him a moment, realizes; laughs*)

GEORGE: Look at that, Marg! Look at Archie! Whooo-
eee!! *OOOO*!! The both of yous: *criers*! If that ain't the
God damndest thing I ever saw! *Whoooo–eee!*

(GEORGE *giggles hysterically.* MARGY *goes to console*
ARCHIE)

MARGY: Archie? Archie, look at me . . . Arch?

ARCHIE: God damn town'll bury ya. . . . You got out,
Margy . . . you and the Moose. . . . Why'd you
come back? Kinda dumb thing to do, Marg, don't you
think? (*Pauses*) I heard you were comin' back. Spike
the Loon showed me the *Item.*

GEORGE (*starting to look through the papers in his wal-
let*): I'm gonna get that . . .

ARCHIE: "Spike," I says, "no way. No way is Margy
Palumbo comin' back to this armpit. No way. She's an
educated woman."

GEORGE: I'll show ya . . . look at this! I kept the clipping from the *Item.* Margaret Burke, *née* Palumbo
. . . this is you . . . Palumbo, and Burke is Moose.

ARCHIE (*grabbing paper*): Gimme that. (*Looks at clipping. To* MARGY) This is you, yes?

MARGY: That is me.

GEORGE: What's the picture in the *Item* for, Margy? Arch? It makes no sense. I read it but it makes no sense.

ARCHIE (*throwing clipping into baler. Completely new attitude*): Let's get this bale finished, huh?

GEORGE: Hey! Picture in the paper for what? What did you do?

ARCHIE: Come on, George! You're not gettin' paid to talk!

(ARCHIE *is now quite energetically loading the baler. He tosses a bundle of newpapers to* GEORGE. GEORGE *grunts under the weight of the bundle*)

GEORGE: Hey!

ARCHIE: I'm balin' paper. If you and this famous woman want to help . . . if you don't want to help, that's fine too. It's what I'm paid to do.

GEORGE: What'd she do, Arch? What'd she get her picture in the paper for? Explain it to me!

ARCHIE (*angrily*): Will you kindly get the bundle in the baler?

GEORGE: I don't like this. (*Pauses*) I'd like to point out to you, Archie, that this Margy Palumbo is tryin' . . . and succeedin' . . . in making God damn fools . . . idiots! . . . outta the rotten two of us.

MARGY: Archie, I'm not doing that.

GEORGE: You think Archie Crisp is just some jerk kid you can fuck over, huh? Fuck him over for a laugh and then scoot right out and spend the next fifteen / twenty years tellin' your highfalutin friends about this local . . . this *local* . . . this townie asshole, Archie Crisp . . . and how he came on to her. Still likin' her and all, after all those years since the second grade. (*Imitates* MARGY *talking to a cultured friend*) "This Archie Crisp, you see, is what you'd call a really steady boyfriend. . . . How steady? Second grade right up till age thirty–five/forty. How's *that* for steady, huh? Those locals stick like glue, huh? Not much goin' in those locals' lives, huh? Couple of farmers, 'ceptin' they got no *farms!*" (*He bales furiously*) She's insulting us, Archie! That's it—she's putting us down!

ARCHIE: Shut it up, George, huh? Huh? Huhhh? You got the brains of a cruller. (*Tosses a bundle into baler*) Leave me out of this. I'm just doing my work.

GEORGE: You're her supper date, right? I mean, she called you, not me. I'm just being friendly and all . . . not comin' on or causin' trouble or nothing' . . . just bein' friendly and all . . . for old time's sake. (*Pauses*) And for the sake of our old buddy Swede . . . who's kicking off . . . (ARCHIE *looks at* GEORGE) Out of memory for the Moose . . . and her former junior high steady, our own Spike the Loon . . . dearly departed . . . and accounta she's got kids, Raymond, et cetera, and her bein' unhappy and all . . . mentally fuckin' *depressed!* (GEORGE *is moving toward* MARGY *now*) We behaved respectably with you on account of all those things, Margy, and what I hear is that you can't stop laughin' at us and

insultin' us and playing it smart . . . playin' it smart
. . . (*He tosses a bundle into the baler*) I've got muscle now, Margy. That's one change from the old days,
right? Me, roly–poly and all. . . . That's one change
you mighta noticed, huh? George Ferguson ain't
roly–poly now! Opposite: George Ferguson is a well–
developed man . . . he's strong . . . he can lift
. . . he's got muscle . . . uh huh. (*He tosses another
bundle into baler. He looks at* ARCHIE) You workin' or
you watchin', huh? If you want a bale wired and out
and ready for your uncle at four o'clock, you gotta
move on it. Same as me . . . (*To* MARGY) I personally
never held with the idea that women are weak and
along for a free ride. (*He throws a bundle to her. It
drops on the floor*) Up and into the baler. MOVE!
(MARGY *hurls bundle at the baler. She grunts angrily*) I do not like the attitude you've got right now!
(GEORGE *shoves* MARGY, *roughly, toward the baler
again*)

ARCHIE: Cool down, George. You're hot . . .

GEORGE: *I'm hot, all right* . . . *I'm hot.* Why not, huh?
How'm I gonna stay cool with Miss Margy Palumbo
blowin' in my ear like she does, huh? (*Turns to*
MARGY, *then to* ARCHIE) This pisses me off. This just
pisses me off. (*Grabs two bundles, throws them into
the baler*) *This just pisses me off* !! (*To* MARGY) What
you're after here is trouble between me and Archie.
That's the way I got it pegged. You get your kicks
outta causin' us to be fightin' and crap with each
other. That's the way I got it pegged . . . (*To* AR-
CHIE) And I got a good eye. I got a good eye. (*To*
MARGY) I don't like the way you call me and Archie
here dumb or stupid for not gettin' our pictures in

the *Item* the way you do . . . (*Displays newspaper photo*) What's this anyway, huh? Does this mean that if anything . . . you know . . . happened to you, that a lot of people would come snoopin' around on accounta you're famous, so's they noticed you were missing kinda thing?

MARGY: My children . . . Raymond and Rosie . . . they'd miss me. . . . They'd "come snoopin'."

GEORGE: I don't like you using your sex on us the way you do . . . to split us up . . . me and my best friend, Archie.

ARCHIE: C'mon already, George . . .

GEORGE: Your fame and your power . . .

ARCHIE: You're talkin' stupid . . .

GEORGE: Your eyelids, blinkin' up and down like you didn't know they were . . . (*Reaches for and grabs* MARGY'*s breasts*) I don't like the way you use these on us, neither . . .

ARCHIE: Keep back . . . less you wanna die young, pal.

GEORGE: It's a little late for either of us "dying young," ain't it, Goat? Dyin' young at our age ain't no more . . . no more . . . (GEORGE *slips around behind* MARGY *and fondles her breasts from behind her*) I don't like the way you've been usin' these on us.

(MARGY *pulls away from* GEORGE *quickly*)

MARGY: George!

ARCHIE: Keep back from her, George, 'less you want to find your nose on your knee in the mornin'! You get me?

GEORGE: What's there to get, Arch, huh? What's there you're saying that's to get? (GEORGE *holds* MARGY *in front of him, gripping her tightly. She is his shield, his hostage*) You wanna come at me, Arch, come on . . . (*Yells*) COME ON!! (GEORGE *flips* MARGY *to one side; squares off with* ARCHIE) COME ON NOW!

(ARCHIE *turns downstage, away from* GEORGE *and* MARGY. *He seems paralyzed by his terror now, frozen. His eyes are wide open, but unfocused: blind.*

GEORGE *is amazed and frightened by* ARCHIE's *state. He snaps his fingers in front of* ARCHIE's *empty eyes.*)

GEORGE: What is *with* you? (*To* MARGY) You see this, Marg? This one's all bark. All bark! Not me. Not me! I got no bark at all, right? No college–boy bullshit, I'm just dumb little Kermie Ferguson from over Gould Street. (*Pauses*) Who gives a shit, huh? Who gives a shit? (*Pauses*) 'Member how we used ta kiss, Marg? The way you used to *tongue* me. Let's show Arch, huh?

(*He kisses her.* MARGY *stands straight, responding stiffly.* GEORGE *breaks away, finds can of beer, swigs; spits in pretended disgust from the touch of* MARGY's *lips*)

GEORGE: You've turned into kinda a dead fish, Marg
. . . (*To* ARCHIE) She's kinda turned into a dead fish
. . . (*Smiles*) Not like the old days, huh? You remember how hot she was, Arch? (*To* MARGY) You remember how hot you were, Bunny?

ARCHIE: C'mon, will ya, George!

GEORGE (*To* MARGY): You ain't in no hoity–toity *Worces-
ter* or no *Springfield* or no *Nooo Yahwk* or no *London,
England* or no *Paris, France* . . . You're in none of
those highfalutin, hoity–toity, swell places now,
Bunny Palumbo! You're home. *Home!* And when
you're home, sistah, you are what you are. (*Pauses;
angrily*) *What you are*!! (*Pauses*) Gangbanged at Fisherman's Beach and she comes up smilin' and beggin'
for more . . . beggin' for more!

ARCHIE: George, for the love of Christ . . . I . . .

(ARCHIE *takes a step toward* GEORGE, *pulls* GEORGE'*s
arm.* GEORGE *pulls away violently.* GEORGE *moves to a
bale and kicks and punches it several times.* MARGY
leans against baler and watches)

GEORGE: No touches! No touches! No touches! (*He
punches bale; turns and faces* MARGY) Gangbanged!
Gangbanged! The whole God damned senior class
party and this one is still smilin' and lookin' for more
. . . (*In a rage; throaty, whispered yell*) Bunny
Palumbo, Blind Swede's sistah . . . Bunny, Bunny,
hop, hop, hop, huh? Right, right? (*Full voice*) Fucks
like a what? Answer me! Fucks like a *what*? ANSWER
ME!

ARCHIE (*from the baler*): Leave her be, George! There's no need ta bring any of this back up!

GEORGE: It's up, it's up! It's already up. (*Moves to AR-CHIE in a rage*) I'll be the one to say what comes up and what doesn't come up! I'll be the one! You get me? *You . . . get . . . me?*

ARCHIE (*almost begging, on the ground*): I don't see the point, that's all. I just don't see the point.

GEORGE: Because this girl forgets who she is, that's why. This girl thinks she can come back to town and be new . . . and she can't . . . she can't. That ain't the way things are. This girl ain't no Princess Margaret . . . this is plain Margy . . . Bunny Palumbo . . . Blind Swede's no–titted sistah . . . our stuck–up Salutatorian. That's who this girl is! This girl is Bunny, the one who got herself gangbanged, senior class beach party, Fisherman's Beach, up Lynn way . . . (*Smiles. He sings*)
Lynn, Lynn:
The city of sin;
You'll never get out,
But, you'll always get in.
(*Moves to* MARGY)
Lynn, Lynn:
The city of sin;
You'll never get out,
But, you'll always get in.
(*Laughs.*)
    Man, oh, man! This is a girl with a *badddd reputation,* ain't that right? . . . Fisherman's Beach, Bunny . . . you remember . . . you remember who went first? You remember? (*Stares at* MARGY) Do you re-

member? (*No reply*) I don't hear an answer . . . (*No reply*) I don't hear an answer . . . (*No reply*) I would like an answer! Do you remember who went first? *Do you remember? Do . . . you . . . remember?*

MARGY (*primal scream*): *You!*

GEORGE (*triumphant*): *Right! Me! Kermie! First!* (*Glares at her, again*) Remember who went second? Do you remember?

MARGY (*weeping*): No.

GEORGE: Think, Bunny, think . . . think. (*Pauses*) *Think!* (*Looks at* ARCHIE) What's wanted here is the memory and name of the man who went second . . . number two . . . sloppy seconds . . . *sloppy seconds* . . . (*Laughs. Looks at* MARGY) Who could that man be? Who, Bunny, who? Try to remember . . . try . . . who? Who? I don't hear an answer . . . who? Who? Who was number two? (*Sing–song; a cheerleader's rhythm*)
Who? Who?
Who was number two!
Who? Who?
Who was number two!
Who? Who?
Who was number two?

ARCHIE (*moaning*): Me!

GEORGE: Another country heard from.

ARCHIE: Me. I was number two. It was me. Don't you remember, Bunny? . . . (*Softly*) Marg? Margy?

Don't you remember? (*Pauses*) It was me, Archie,
Billy–Goat Crisp. (*Pauses*) I was talkin' to you all the
way . . . all the way. I went all the way . . . talkin'
to you . . . whisperin' in your ear . . . tellin' you "I
love you, Marg." (*Pauses*) I did. (*Bows his head*) I do.

GEORGE (*laughing*): This is terrific! Whooooo–eeeee!
(*Pauses; softly, simply*) This is terrific. (GEORGE *walks
about in two large circles, forming a figure eight. He
is quite pleased with himself. He turns to* MARGY
suddenly) Three! Number Three!

ARCHIE: God damn you!

GEORGE: Three, Bunny, three!

ARCHIE: Don't do this, George.

GEORGE:
Number three, number three.
Who d'ya see?
Number three . . .

Number three, number three . . .
Who d'ya see?
Number three . . .
(*Giggling*)
I don't hear an answer, Bunny–baby . . .

MARGY (*simply, softly*): Peter . . . (*Pauses*) Swede
. . . my brother . . .

GEORGE: You got it, Bunny! You got it! (*Laughs; walks in
figure eight again*) This is terrific, huh, Arch? Isn't
this terrific?

ARCHIE: Yuh. You got it, George. Terrific. (ARCHIE *looks at* MARGY. *Their eyes meet*) Why did ya have ta call me? Couldn't you have stayed away? (*Pauses*) Jesus, Margy . . . (*Looks away, extremely upset*) Jesus.

GEORGE: Number four, Margy?

MARGY (*softly*): Cootie Webber . . .

GEORGE: Are you kidding me? Or what? Cootie Webber? Number four? Nothin' like that . . . Spike the Loon was number four. Porker Watson was number five and Stoney Webster was number six. (*Pauses*) Cootie Webber was number seven. (*Smiles*) Me and Spike the Loon went over the lineup, couldn'ta be'n more'n three weeks ago. (*Pauses*) I led off, Archie was sloppy seconds. Swede was *numero trez* and Spike the Loon was the definite clean–up. (*Pauses*) Cootie Webber was number seven. (*Pauses*) Cootie Webber was the Moose's best friend, Marg, you remember? Asshole buddies, first grade right up ta graduation, all twelve years. I myself personally always knew Moose Burke was a complete shithead, but who woulda guessed he woulda gone for the town pump, huh? (*To* ARCHIE) Married her. Jee–zus! God damn married her! What a shithead, huh? If that ain't the most disgusting thing I've ever seen! Billy–Goat Crisp, crying like a girl. (*Whistles*) God damn. (*Pauses: new attitude*) God damn . . . (GEORGE *walks in a figure eight now. His bottom lip trembles as he fights back the tears*) What I can't believe here is that you let this one do it to us over and over again . . . (*To* MARGY) He couldn't stand it that I went first. Ya know what I mean? (*Circling her now*) He pestered me for years. I don't know what for. I mean, ya can't take a true fact

and change it . . . just to do away with somebody's
jealousy, right? (*Pauses*) I went first and he went second. Kermie led off and Billy–Goat took what was
left. (*Pauses*) I foxed him, Marg. (*To* ARCHIE, *who is
still weeping*) Didn't I fox you? (*To* MARGY) He was
s'pose ta go first. It was all his idea . . . at Fisherman's Beach . . . the love–makin' . . . with you,
Marg. That was all Archie's idea . . . (*Smiles*) You
can read all the books you want and speak all the
languages goin', Marg, and you ain't *never* . . .
never . . . you ain't never gonna live that one down.
(*Pauses*) Ain't that a fact? Ain't it? (*Pauses*) Sure . . .
(*To* ARCHIE) Ain't it a fact, Arch? She ain't never livin'
that one down, right? (*To* MARGY) See? Talking about
it doesn't bother me at all, sistah!

MARGY (*quietly, at first*): I'm hardly your sister, George.
In respect to my dear family, I must say, the implication is just hideous.

GEORGE: I don't like your mouth.

MARGY (*in a sudden rage, she spits her words. Wakefield accent. She is the teenaged "toughie" she once
was*): THEN WHY'D YOU GO AND STICK YOUR
TONGUE IN IT?! (*She dances her rage about*) C'mon,
ya blow'ah! C'mon, ya blow'ah! Ya wanna hit a girrlll?
Huh? Huh? Huh? C'mon. C'mon, c'mon . . . ya look
wicked stooopid, George. (*She takes the stage. Her
accent has suddenly returned to normal; as does her
manner. Her rage is her own*) I was seventeen,
George, seventeen. Do you know how old seventeen
is, George? Not very. *Not God damn very!* Do you
have any idea what it was you stuck into my seventeen–year–old MIND, George? Do you? *Do you?*

(*Pauses*) "Why'd they pick me? Was I too provoca-
tive? Was it the way I smiled? Did I look available?
Did I look like an easy lay?" (*Pauses*) What was it,
George? What was it about me that you hated . . .
so deeply . . . so completely . . . so absolutely . . .
that made you want to *make love,* hmmm? (*Pauses*)
Years, God damn *years* of walking around like a zom-
bie, wondering was I really, deep down, underneath
it all, *lookin' for it?* I remember, ya' know, George. I
really do. I was kinda standing off by myself, pitch
black out, no moon at all . . . and alls'a'sudden
somebody turns me around and kisses me. I pull back
from him, tryin' ta laugh it off, I say, "No, thanks,
really . . ." and he's giggling this kinda' high–
pitched girlish giggle. (*She imitates* GEORGE's *giggle,
then suddenly moves to* GEORGE, *faces him, eyeball
to eyeball*) Weren't you giggling, Kermie, huh? And
you hit me. You took your hand and you hit me. I
square off with him . . . with this Kermie Ferguson
blow'ah, 'cause I ain't a'scared of nobody. *No . . .
fucking . . . body!* (*She is now atop mound of newspapers: the sand dune*) Seventeen years old, five–
foot–one–inch . . . and you hit me. And I whack you
back and you hit me and you hit me and I fall over
backwards and you hit me and then you and your
kind did what you did. You line up . . . *LINE UP*
. . . and you did what you did!

GEORGE: You loved it.

MARGY (*crossing to steps in front of baler; squares off
with* GEORGE. *In a rage: Wakefield accent*): I DID
NOT LOVE IT! I HATED IT! I HATED IT! (*Crying
as she screams, the Massachusetts accent thickens,
dominates her speech*) You know what I was doing,

you jerks?! You know what I was doin' while you was doin' it to me? Huh? Huh? HUH? (*Laughs*) I was thinking that I was getting run over . . . by a bus . . . by the *Hudson* bus. That's what I was doin', I swear ta Christ! That's how much I *loved it*! (*Dancing in her raging state, she imitates*) "Oooooooo, Arch!" . . . . "Studie–doo" . . . I liked Swede . . . "Yo, Margyyyy! Open 'em up! Spread 'em out! Here comes *love*!"

GEORGE: Is this what you came back here for, ya bitch? Ta get even with us?

MARGY: You bet your ass I'm gonna get even! Yuh, George, yessireebob! I'm gonna get even. I am! Wicked awful even! I'm gonna get sooo even with you, George, I can taste it! Taste . . . it!

(MARGY *turns her back.* GEORGE *giggles nervously, looks down.* ARCHIE *calls out to* MARGY *quietly*)

ARCHIE: The only reason I got inta line, Margy, was 'cause I didn't think you'd have me any other way. I was never good enough, Marg . . . never smart enough . . . never sophisticated like you were. . . . That's why, Marg. Ever since the second grade I've carried a torch for ya . . . som'pin' wicked . . .

GEORGE: "Ever since the second grade . . ." Jesus!

ARCHIE: Nobody planned it, Margy. It just happened! Honest ta God! I mean, well, boys are always talkin' about wantin' ta do it with this one or that one . . .

and *everybody* was always sayin' they'd love ta do it
with *you*, 'cause you were, well, beautiful. But nobody really *meant* it: jumpin' you. It's just when
George, here, well, *started*, everybody . . . wanted
to, too. Everybody liked you . . .

MARGY: You *"liked"* me, Arch?

ARCHIE: I did. A lot.

MARGY: And that's how you showed me you *"liked"*
me?

ARCHIE: I was tricked out of first, I was. Otherwise,
Margy, the first words you woulda heard whispered
in your ear woulda been "I love you" . . . because I
did and I do. I do still. Marg . . . som'pin'
wicked . . .

MARGY (*after a long pause; calmly*): "I love you" would
not have helped. Do you have any idea what my
dreams were like for the first, say, three and a half
years after our senior class celebration? (*Pauses*) You
think I really missed our reunions, Arch? Really? I
had one a night—in my dreams—for three and a half
years . . . 365 nights a year for three and a half
years. That's a shitload of getting–together, don't you
agree? (*Sternly*) Don't you agree? (*No reply. She
screams at them*) Don't you agree? (*She stands her
ground now, staring directly at* ARCHIE *and at*
GEORGE. ARCHIE *bows his head;* GEORGE *giggles. She
swallows a sob; pauses. She speaks to* ARCHIE, *quietly,
excluding* GEORGE *at first*) I had no plan to get even,
Archie: none. I took this trip home because my

brother Peter took what they call in the medical game "a turn for the worst." He's extremely weak, extremely frail, extremely close to the end. The doctors told me Peter wouldn't be able to talk to me. But as soon as I sat next to him, he talked. He has a strong memory of our beach party. He wept and he begged my forgiveness. I gave Peter my forgiveness and it made him feel "wick'd good." It made me feel "wick'd good," too. Call me crazy, but I kinda figured you guys'd be begging my forgiveness, too. But the truth is, after having this little first reunion fellas, I would like to kill both of you. I would very much like to watch both of you suffer and die: be dead. (ARCHIE *moans;* GEORGE *giggles*) It looks like Getting–even is just the kinda guy I am.

ARCHIE: I, uh, I, uh, 'm sorry, Marg. I really am. I never thought what was done was a good thing. I never thought that. I am . . . uh . . . well . . . ashamed. I wish it never happened. I wish there was a way of takin' it back 'cause I would. I'm awful sorry, Marg, I am. But I gotta tell ya som'pin': What they did was *dirty,* Marg. What I did was *making love,* and that's the truth. I've never loved another woman besides you, Marg. Not even one. I'm beggin' ya to believe me and to forgive me.

GEORGE (*in disgust*): He loves Bunny Palumbo, this Billy–Goat does.

MARGY (*glaring at* GEORGE, *momentarily; then to* AR-CHIE): I believe you, Archie . . . and I forgive you, Archie, I do. (MARGY *cradles* ARCHIE's *head, watching* GEORGE *as she does. She prods* GEORGE *into ac-*

tion) Do you see this, George? I've just forgiven Archie.

GEORGE: I don't like this . . . you're just forgivin' him: not me, too? (*Pauses*) Stay back from him, Bunny. (*Steps toward them*) You hear me?

MARGY: You're not splitting us up, George. I choose my date for the twentieth, Archie: you. I do . . .

ARCHIE: Really?

GEORGE (*Genuinely upset, runs at* ARCHIE *and kicks him between legs, from behind.* GEORGE *now faces* MARGY): You think you can just hop back inta town and be another person from what you are? You are who you are, Bunny, hop, hop, huh? Huh? (GEORGE *unhitches his belt*) What I want here is what you gave my friend about an hour ago. (*Advancing toward* MARGY) What's wanted here is more love-makin' . . .

MARGY (*hitting* GEORGE): Put it out of your mind, George . . .

GEORGE: It's already *in* my mind!

(*He moves to* MARGY, *who slaps his face again violently. He reels backward*)

MARGY: Don't you lay a hand on me . . . ever . . . *ever*! Not a hand . . . not an eye . . . not a word . . . (*She slaps his face*) From you. . . . Nothing is wanted, George Ferguson . . . (*She slaps his face*) Nothing!

GEORGE (*feeling his cheek. He is next to* ARCHIE *now, who is standing, head bowed*): Every time you hit me, Marg, I'm hitting this one.

(GEORGE *backhands* ARCHIE, *who screams in pain*)

MARGY: God damn you! (*She slaps* GEORGE)

GEORGE (*backhanding* ARCHIE *again*): I don't even like you *talkin'* to me, Marg!

MARGY: What have they done to you, George? What have they done to you to make you so incredibly dumb? (MARGY *hits* GEORGE. GEORGE *backhands* AR-CHIE) Have they beaten you? Have you been tor-tured? (*She hits* GEORGE *again*. GEORGE *backhands* ARCHIE *again*) I'd like you to stop it now, George. Put your hand at your side . . . George? Did you hear me? I don't want you to raise your hand to Archie again. Put your hand down, George. (GEORGE *smiles. He suddenly, without breaking his stare at* MARGY, *hits* ARCHIE *with the back of his hand, dealing a terrible blow*) George!

(MARGY *swings at* GEORGE, *who shoves her aside.* MARGY *falls on to her back on the mound of old news-papers. It looks as though* GEORGE *will rape her*)

GEORGE: Nothin' changes, Margy . . . (*He pulls her up to her feet, her back to audience*) Nothin' changes. Not around here. Nothin' . . . (*He rips her blouse open. She is barebreasted. Her naked shoulders glis-ten against the filth of the old newspaper, against the filth of* GEORGE's *leering, hateful stare*) I knew it! I *fuckin' knew it* ! (*To* ARCHIE) No underwear on top!

You see this, Arch? (*Yells*) Do . . . you . . . see . . .
this?? (*To* MARGY) No shame. No shame, you. No
shame. (ARCHIE *pulls himself up from the ground
and moves toward* GEORGE, *stands square with him*)
Hey, Arch, c'mon, huh? . . . You look wicked awful
pissed off at me . . .

(ARCHIE *grabs* GEORGE. *The two large men wrestle.*
GEORGE *gains an advantage, shoving* ARCHIE *atop a
low bale.* GEORGE *runs to baler, finds tool box and
grabs a hammer. He swings head of hammer against
front of baler, as* ARCHIE *advances toward him: a warning.*

ARCHIE *moves in.* GEORGE *swings hammer at* ARCHIE's
head. ARCHIE *ducks under, lifting* GEORGE *high over
his head.*

GEORGE *crashes the hammer down on the baler's steel
steps.*

ARCHIE *rolls* GEORGE *onto floor, twisting* GEORGE's
arm, forcing GEORGE *to drop hammer to cement floor.*

ARCHIE *throws* GEORGE *across stage into bale of corrugated cardboard, face first.* GEORGE *rolls onto mound
of old newspapers.* GEORGE *rises up on his knees, confused.* ARCHIE *butts* GEORGE *with the top of his head.*
GEORGE *falls over into pit backwards, stunned, hurt
badly*)

ARCHIE (*To* MARGY, *with a madman's rational voice*):
800–pound bales . . . eight of 'em ta fill Uncle Max's
truck. Been doin' it for years now . . . since I was a
kid. (ARCHIE *moves downstage; talks again to* MARGY

in a mysteriously calm fashion, given the situation)
What we do is buy up old paper, bale it and truck the
bales up to the mills and sell them . . . up Fitchburg
. . . Ayer . . . Shirley. (ARCHIE *goes to* GEORGE *and
kicks him in the stomach. He then chases* GEORGE
behind baler and kicks GEORGE *with a terrible blow.*
GEORGE *then flies back into the audience's view, upstage right, into stack of bales.* ARCHIE *returns to*
MARGY, *downstage, continuing his explanation of
his quandary about his life's labor. He is terribly
upset)* They buy our paper and they process it, see?
And they make it into paper. Use ta bother me that I
was workin' so hard takin' paper to people who were
makin' paper . . . I mean, it never seemed like too
much of a life bringin' paper all's the way up ta Fitchburg, just so's they could make more paper. I mean,
what's the world gonna do with so much paper, any-
how?

(Suddenly, silently, GEORGE *pulls himself up and circles behind baler on catlike toes. He clears his blurred
vision, focuses on* ARCHIE. *He then runs straight at*
ARCHIE, *grabbing* ARCHIE *in a headlock)*

MARGY: Archie!

GEORGE *(desperately)*: Billy–Goat gonna die.

ARCHIE: *Leggo . . . my . . . head! Leggo!* (ARCHIE *re-
lives his prophetic story of Lum by running* GEORGE
backwards, upstage, then flipping GEORGE *into baler
face first.* GEORGE'*s face "explodes," blood suddenly
erupting, staining front door of baler.* GEORGE *falls
away, upstage, face down on mound of old newspapers.* MARGY *bows her head, leaning against a bale,*

facing the men. ARCHIE *runs in panic, ratlike, in quick little figure eights, from* GEORGE *to* MARGY *and then to the loading door, all the way upstage. When he reaches the loading doors, he stops and calls to* MARGY. GEORGE'*s blood is visible on front of baler, like Oriental brush–painting)* George . . . all bloody, Margy. . . . We're in trouble . . . Margy . . . run . . . run, Margy, run, run, Margy, run, run, run . . . (MARGY *goes silently to George, looks at him. She then looks at blood on baler door. She touches blood, pulling her hand down through stain, enlarging it.* MARGY *goes to locker; collects her jacket, scarf, sweater, purse.* ARCHIE *runs around back of baler, downstage, calls across to* MARGY, *begs her to leave)* Please, Margy, run, run. Don't be dead. Run, Margy, please, run, please?

(MARGY *moves a few steps toward* ARCHIE, *stops when she makes eye contact with* ARCHIE; *speaks)*

MARGY (*simply, clearly*): I'll be back, Archie. It's a long list.

(MARGY *moves directly to loading doors, exits the play, slamming door behind her.*

ARCHIE *is stunned, unmoving. He runs in ratlike half–circle to loading doors, as if to prove to himself that* MARGY *is really gone. He again moves to the fallen* GEORGE)

ARCHIE: Kermie? Kermie? C'mon, Kermie, we gotta run. Kermie? It's Billy–Goat. Kermie? (*Rolls* GEORGE *over; sees that* GEORGE *is dead. Groans)* Oh, Jesus! Archie Crisp just killed Georgie Ferguson and there's gonna be wicked awful hell ta pay . . . (*Returns to* GEORGE) (ARCHIE *lifts* GEORGE's *arm and tries to coax* GEORGE *back into life. He drags* GEORGE *by the feet to front of baler*) This ain't funny, Kermie, ya dumb blow'ah. . . . C'mon, huh? This here's wicked awful scarey, Kerm! Kermie! We gotta run, Kermie, together, huh? I don't wanna run withoutcha, so's ya better hurry. (ARCHIE *covers* GEORGE *with old newspapers*) Oh, Jesus! Kermie? Kermie? Don't be dead, Kermie, don't be dead! Don't be dead! (*Screams*) *DON'T BE DEAD!* (ARCHIE *stands, back to baler, the mound that is* GEORGE's *newspaper–covered dead body at* ARCHIE's *feet.* ARCHIE's *breathing is loud, labored, rythmical.* ARCHIE *stares straight out into auditorium. His eyes are dead, hollow. It is the stare of a blind man. He breathes deeply, four audible breaths. All lights fade out, but for single worklight overhead.* ARCHIE's *breathing stops. There is a moment of absolute silence*)

Sudden blackout

The play is over.

ISRAEL HOROVITZ (*Playwright*) was born in Wakefield, Massachusetts, in 1939. His first play, "The Comeback," was written at age seventeen. In the thirty-three years that have followed, nearly 50 Horovitz plays have been translated and performed in as many as 20 languages worldwide. Among the best–known Horovitz plays are: "The Indian Wants The Bronx," which introduced Al Pacino and John Cazale; "Line," which introduced Richard Dreyfuss (a revival of "Line" is now entering its fifteenth year, off–Broadway); "It's Called The Sugar Plum," which introduced Marsha Mason and Jill Clayburgh; "Rats;" "Morning" of the Horovitz–McNally–Melfi triptych, "Morning, Noon and Night;" "The Wakefield Plays," a seven–play cycle including "Hopscotch," "The 75th," "Alfred The Great," "Our Father's Failing," "Alfred Dies," "Stage Directions" and "Spared;" "Mackerel;" "The Primary English Class," which starred Diane Keaton in its NYC premiere; and "The Good Parts." For the past several years, Mr. Horovitz has been at work on a cycle of plays set in his adopted hometown, Gloucester, Massachusetts, all of which have had their world premieres at The Gloucester Stage Company, a theatre founded by Horovitz ten years ago, and which he still serves as its Artistic Director/Producer. Among Horovitz's Gloucester plays are: "The Widow's Blind Date," which played to SRO audiences for several months at The Gloucester Stage Company, and re–opened in NYC off–Broadway in December, 1989; "Park Your Car In Harvard Yard," which was workshopped at the Manhattan Theatre Club with Burgess Meredith and Ellen Burstyn, and recently triumphed in Paris; "Henry

Lumper," which was a success off–Broadway in 1989; "North Shore Fish," which was a hit at the WPA Theatre off–Broadway and is slated for transfer to Broadway this coming fall; 1988's Hudson Guild Theatre entry, "Yes Of The Duck;" "Firebird At Dogtown;" "Fighting Over Beverly," which was commissioned by England's Hampstead Theatre Company, where the play will have its premiere next season; and "Sunday Runners In The Rain," which was workshopped at The N.Y. Shakespeare Festival. He has just completed a new Gloucester–based play, "Strong–Man's Weak Child," which he will direct at the Los Angeles Theatre Center in May 1990. Other recent Horovitz plays include "The Former One–On–One Basketball Champion," which was produced last season in Seattle, starring former Boston Celtics great, Bill Russell; and Horovitz's "Sault Ste. Marie Trilogy:" "Today, I Am A Fountain Pen;" "A Rosen By Any Other Name;" and "The Chopin Playoffs." His short comedy "Faith" was seen off–Broadway in the Horovitz–McNally–Melfi reunion triptych, "Faith, Hope and Charity." Horovitz has recently completed four original screenplays: "The Deuce;" "Payofski's Discovery;" "The Pan;" and "Letters to Iris." He is currently adapting "Strong–Man's Weak Child" for the screen. Other films written by Horovitz include "The Strawberry Statement;" "Believe In Me;" "Author! Author!" and "A Man In Love" (written with Diane Kurys). Horovitz has won numerous awards, including the Obie (twice), the Emmy, Prix du Plaisir de Theatre (for "Line" in Paris), Prix du Jury (Cannes Film Festival), the New York Drama Desk Award, an Award in Literature of The American Academy of Arts and Letters and the Eliot Norton Prize. He is America's most–produced living playwright in France. In French theatre history, only one other American, Eugene O'Neill, has had more plays translated and produced in the

French language. Horovitz is married to Gillian Adams, the former British National Marathon Champion, and is the father of five children, film producers Rachael and Matthew, Beastie Boys rock–star/actor Adam, and Hannah and Oliver Horovitz, unemployed 4–year–old twins. The Horovitz family divides its time among homes in Gloucester, Massachusetts, NYC's Greenwich Village, and London's Dulwich Village.

March, 1990